PRAISE FOR

WORDS TO LIVE BY

"This rare and valuable gift is a gentle introduction to serious Bible study that takes seriously the details essential to a proper vantage of the paradigmatic portraits in Scripture. With unprecedented credentials for a project of this scope and purpose, this mother-daughter writing team has created an intelligent and effective tool that should serve the church for years to come. With word studies and topical reflections, from 'Abba' to 'Zealous,' this substantive volume sets forth a beginning vocabulary for those new to the Christian faith while it 'reminds' more seasoned followers of the grammar of Christianity. Suitable for private study and small group resource."

—**David Fleer,** Professor of Homiletics & Special Asst. to the President, Director of the Thomas H. Olbricht Christian Scholars' Conference

"*Words to Live By* is not only a delightful study, but very helpful. Ann and Nancy invite us to slow down and taste the delight of meaningful biblical words that deeply enrich our Christian walk. This is particularly helpful in a time when language is used so carelessly. The organization of this book makes it a practical and powerful personal devotional resource as well as a valuable guide for small group study. Don't fail to read carefully the concluding 'next step' suggestions!"

—**Earl D. Lavender,** Director of Missional Studies, Lipscomb University

"A great resource for individual and group study. This book brings the words to life! The authors' desire to stay true to God's Word and expand the knowledge of application for spiritual growth is a blessing for all who seek to find the Truth in the biblical text."

—**Dr. Phil Vardiman,** Elder, Hillcrest Church of Christ, Professor of Business Management, Abilene Christian University

"If you want to discover the deeper, richer meaning of Bible words, this book is for you! *Words to Live By*, by Nancy Ferguson and Ann Doyle, lives up to its subtitle: *A Readers' Guide to Key Bible Terms*. These 34 words include *Areopagus/Mars' Hill*, *perfect* (meaning 'complete' or 'mature'), and *mystery* (meaning 'something revealed'). Each insightfully concludes with the infusion of meditation and application through questions, prayer, and Scripture."

—**Dr. Cynthia Guy,** author of *What About the Women?* and *Struggle. Seek. Grow.*

"Discovering a resource that functions both as a devotional and as a dictionary refreshes the soul. Nancy and Ann strike a beautiful balance with easy-to-read applicability on one hand and sound scholarship on the other. Perfect for both personal use and small group settings, this is a must-read for those who seek a deeper level of understanding of Scripture without sacrificing readability and practicality."

—**Geoff Carroll,** Teacher/Owner of Travel the Text

WORDS
TO LIVE BY

WORDS
TO LIVE BY

A READER'S GUIDE TO KEY BIBLE TERMS

NANCY FERGUSON
& ANN DOYLE

LEAFWOOD
PUBLISHERS
an imprint of Abilene Christian University Press

WORDS TO LIVE BY

A Reader's Guide to Key Bible Terms

LEAFWOOD
P U B L I S H E R S
an imprint of Abilene Christian University Press

Copyright © 2017 by Nancy Ferguson and Ann Doyle

ISBN 978-1-68426-030-0

Printed in the United States of America

Library of Congress Cataloging-in-Publication Data is on file at the Library of Congress,
Washington DC.

Cover design by ThinkPen Design, LLC
Interior text design by Strong Design, Sandy Armstrong

Leafwood Publishers is an imprint of Abilene Christian University Press
ACU Box 29138
Abilene, Texas 79699

1-877-816-4455
www.leafwoodpublishers.com

17 18 19 20 21 22 / 7 6 5 4 3 2 1

I and Pangur Ban my cat,
'Tis a like task we are at:
Hunting mice is his delight,
Hunting words I sit all night.

Oftentimes a mouse will stray
In the hero Pangur's way;
Oftentimes my keen thought set
Takes a meaning in its net.

Practice every day has made
Pangur perfect in his trade;
I get wisdom day and night
Turning darkness into light

—from Gaelic poem by a 9th century Irish monk in the
Reichenau Primer (which also includes texts on Latin and
Greek grammar); translation by Robin Flower

To our readers,
who also delight in catching words

CONTENTS

A BEGINNING

I grew up in a home built by loving parents devoted to the study and teaching of God's word and in a church that believed the Bible should be the source of our faith and practice. It was years before I realized how odd my childhood was. My introduction to Greek, the language of the New Testament, was my father writing words on a blackboard in our attic playroom and explaining them to my brother and sister and me. We giggled and joked about how they looked and sounded, but soon learned enough to recognize words in the Greek Bible, and to use a Greek dictionary. He was as happy sharing his knowledge with us as he was teaching graduate students at the university. When I was barely a teenager, his research on backgrounds of the New Testament took us all to Greece for a semester, where we visited many of the places mentioned in the Bible—sometimes being given a tour by the archaeologist who had excavated the site. My introduction to church history was in a class he taught for a small mission church in Athens. Later, I majored in Bible in college—as my mother had—and studied biblical languages. I knew her basic knowledge of Greek had been helpful to her in teaching Bible classes and in writing Bible teaching material, but I gained a new respect for her when she typed papers for me (pre-computer days) and corrected my Greek accents!

So much in the world of scholarship can be of great value in Bible study, but it is somewhat inaccessible to many Christians. I hope that this book may help make some of that value available in the church beyond the university.

ANN DOYLE

In my first book, *Living a Worthy Life*, I discussed several topics in which a better understanding of biblical teachings helps us to live the worthy life God wants us to live. The subjects chosen were not ones that are difficult or disputed, but simply ones I realized I needed to study further; so I thought others might also benefit from studying them. A more careful examination of various verses on each of the topics helps to clarify our understanding and draws us into a more meaningful relation-ship with the Lord.

In a similar way, *For the Love of the Lord* explored the mean-ing of love and biblical teaching on love, as it relates to various aspects of our lives. The book defined biblical *agape* love and considered how that love works out in various relationships.

In this volume, I want to explain specific words that are important in the Bible but often are not well understood. There are many words that have a different meaning in everyday speech than the meaning they have in biblical usage (such as "hope," "passion," and "mystery") or that are unfamiliar outside of religious use (like "edify," "hosanna," and "atoning sacrifice"). Discovering the deeper, richer meaning of these words helps us to understand better the message of the passages where they are used and allows us to make the connections between Scripture and life.

Although I have studied some Greek, I knew I would need help on this book; therefore, I asked my daughter to collaborate with me. She majored in biblical languages in college, and she has continued to study and teach Bible classes for all ages. We have now worked together on this book for several years—and we still love each other!

Nancy Ferguson

This book was written with the firm conviction that the Bible is the inspired Word of God, and that it contains all the information necessary for salvation and Christian living. If you are a new Christian, we write to you because you have come to salvation. You may be unfamiliar with the language of faith, but you are eager to know what it means to follow Christ. If you have been a Christian for some time, we write to you because the Word of God lives in you. You want to understand the Bible better and are looking for help to learn all that God would teach you. If you are a Bible teacher, we write to you because you know the Eternal God. You are seeking to reveal the mysteries of Scripture to the world, and the Holy Spirit guides you in this work.

There are many ways to study the Bible. It has historical value. It has great literary merit. It has endless possibilities for devotional meditation. But for a Christian, its greatest value is as the Word of God, telling us who God is, who we are, and how we should live. This book is designed as a gentle introduction to serious Bible study.

When one looks at a piece of art, one first gets an overall impression of what it is—for example, a picture of a woman with intriguing eyes and smile. On continued examination, each person sees the woman a little differently because they bring something of themselves and their own experience to the art—is she content or lonely, remembering or planning? The work can also be studied for the details of the landscape in the background, the position of her hands, and the drape of her clothing. These details together make up the picture, and yet they can each be studied on their own merit.

In this book we are focusing on some of the smaller details of Bible study—the meaning of individual words. Sometimes one should read long passages to identify the themes and the overall message. Other times one should study the details that make up that big picture; these details are the focus of this book. When a child first learns to read, each word must be carefully studied and learned. Eventually, the teacher will encourage the child to use the context to guess the meaning of unfamiliar words in order to progress through a paragraph smoothly. As adults, we often assume we fully understand the meaning of familiar words we guessed long ago; however, it can be enlightening to pause and make use of a dictionary or online resources to explore the full range of meanings of a particular word.

Each person will read the Bible a little differently, because each person has a different background and different experiences. But of course, Scripture is more than just great literature.

> First of all you must understand this, that no prophecy of scripture is a matter of one's own interpretation, because no prophecy ever came by the impulse of man, but men moved by the Holy Spirit spoke from God. (2 Pet. 1:20–21 RSV)

This book was written with confidence that the Bible is the inspired Word of God, and that it is as relevant for us today as it was for those who received it when it was written. Its message of salvation is simple enough for anyone to read and understand. And yet, one can devote a lifetime to studying the Bible and still discover new treasures every day.

In order to discover more of the treasures of the Bible, this book will sometimes discuss the words used in the original languages of the Bible, not just the English words used to translate them. (Often we use italics in the Bible quotations to indicate which English words are used to translate the Greek term under consideration.) Don't worry if you don't know anything about Greek or Hebrew—the words will be explained. But if you do already know a little, then by all means practice what you know—look up the words in a lexicon and read the passages in the original languages. Use the occasion to learn more.

We encourage you to read each entry in order and to spend some time with the suggestions for further study that follow each one. The words are arranged in alphabetical order to make them easy to locate if you have questions about a particular word. If you are using this book with a group, some of the further study questions should provoke interesting conversations; others will require the use of various study aids (such as a concordance), which may be in the form of books or online resources; none require advanced preparation, although some participants may prefer to study individually before discussing together. The final question in each section is designed for private study after the others are completed.

It is our prayer that God will bless each of you in this study, and in your continuing journey of faith.

NANCY & ANN

ABBA

And by him we cry, "Abba, Father."

The New Testament was written in Greek, the language of commerce at that time, understood and spoken throughout the Mediterranean world and beyond. For most who spoke Greek, it was not their first language; some other language was the language of the heart used with family and closest friends. For many in the land where Jesus walked, Aramaic was their first language. Aramaic and Hebrew are written with the same alphabet, but they are different languages. (Similarly, French and Italian are separate languages that use the same alphabet.) There are several Aramaic words used in the Greek New Testament, and "Abba" is one of them. It is the word by which small children call their fathers. It will probably be the first or second word that a baby learns to say. It connects the baby with the father.

Aramaic now has only about half a million speakers (mostly among endangered populations of Iran, Iraq, and Syria). However, it used to be the main language in the Middle East. It was the official language of the Assyrian Empire that conquered the northern kingdom of Israel (2 Kings 17:1–24). It was also the language of trade used by all of the countries that had dealings with Assyria. Aramaic was the language of the Babylonian Empire that conquered Assyria and the southern kingdom of Judah (2 Kings 24:10–17). Daniel and Esther would have spoken Aramaic as captives in Babylon, and parts of the books of Daniel (2:4–7:28) and Ezra (4:8–6:16; 7:12–26) were written in Aramaic instead of in Hebrew like most of the Old Testament. Hebrew and Aramaic are similar in many ways, and for a long time both languages would have been spoken in Israel. After a remnant of the Jews returned from Babylonian captivity to rebuild Jerusalem (2 Chron. 36:20–23; Ezra 1:1–6), Aramaic became the primary language in Israel. Jewish men still learned Hebrew so that they could read the Scriptures, but Aramaic was the language they usually spoke with their friends and family. When Ezra read God's laws to the assembly of exiles who had returned to Jerusalem (Neh. 8:1–12) the reading would have been in Hebrew and the explanation (verse 12) in Aramaic. Aramaic would have been Jesus's first language and the one in which most of his teaching was done.

Although some suggest "Abba" was the equivalent of the English word "Daddy," there is not an exact correspondence. "Abba" still carried a sense of respect—more like "Father" rather than the familiarity of "Daddy." However, the word does suggest the closeness and affection of a family relationship.

Spanish "Appa" and Italian "Papa" may have a similar mix of affection and respect.

The Aramaic word "Abba" is used three times in the New Testament: Mark 14:36, Romans 8:15, and Galatians 4:6. As Jesus prayed to his father in the Garden of Gethsemane on the night of his betrayal and arrest, he addressed God by praying, "Abba, Father" (Mark 14:36). Even though he was an adult, he called his father by the name a child might use. He felt the warm connection that exists between a loving father and a well-loved and loving son.

Each of the four Gospels opens with recognition that Jesus is the Son of God: Matthew, with the angel telling Joseph that Mary conceived by the Holy Spirit (1:20); Mark, with the voice from heaven acknowledging Jesus as "my Son whom I love" at his baptism (1:11); Luke, with an angel telling Mary she will give birth to "the Son of the Most High" (1:32); and John, with the statement "the Word was God . . . in him was life . . ." (1:1, 4) and with the testimony of John the Baptizer at Jesus's baptism that "this is the Son of God" (1:34). Matthew (3:17) and Luke (3:22) also record Jesus's baptism and God's public affirmation on that occasion that Jesus is his son.

What could be more amazing than the Son of God born as a human? And yet, there is more. Through Jesus, we too may become children of God. In Romans 8:14–17, Paul uses "Abba" to show that Christians are children of God and joint heirs with Christ. The privilege of addressing God by the child's term "Abba" is given only to the children of the Father, including not just Jesus, but also those children who are adopted.

In Galatians 4:6, Paul again used "Abba" to show that Christians are God's children, and so, his heirs:

But when the right time came, God sent his Son, who was born from a woman and lived under the law. God did this so that he could buy the freedom of those who were under the law. God's purpose was to make us his children. Since you are now God's children, he has sent the Spirit of his Son into your hearts. The Spirit cries out, "Abba, Father." Now you are not slaves like before. You are God's children, and you will receive everything he promised his children. (Gal. 4:4–7 ERV)

Through union with Christ and reception of his Spirit, Christians have the privilege of addressing God using the same terms as did Jesus, as well-loved children.

Questions and Reflection

Can you think of songs that that address God as "Father"? Songs of praise or prayer songs?

Read the following Old Testament Scriptures portraying God as a father. Whose Father is he, and what is the meaning behind the image each time?

Isaiah 64:8   Malachi 1:6
Jeremiah 31:20   (See also Acts 17:28–29)

Read John 5:17–18 where Jesus refers to God as Father. What is different about his use of this image?

Each person's relationship with his or her own father will influence that person's understanding of God as a father. In what ways might this be a negative picture? In what ways might this be positive? Is the idea of God as Father used as a positive or negative image in Scripture?

There are many passages where God is described in human terms. In each of the following Scriptures, what is the image used to describe God, and what is the main point being made about God by the use of that particular picture?

1 Samuel 8:6–7	Isaiah 54:5–8
Psalm 22:9–10	Isaiah 59:16–17
Isaiah 5:4–5	Jeremiah 18:3–6
Isaiah 40:10–11	Ezekiel 18:30
Isaiah 49:15	Luke 13:20–21

What does the reference to Jesus as the "first-born among many brethren" in Romans 8:29 RSV say about a Christian's relationship to God and to Jesus?

What do each of the following verses say about how one becomes part of the family of God?

John 3:5   Romans 6:4
Ephesians 1:4–8   Titus 3:4–7

Prayer
Use Jude 1:17–22 to pray for yourself and
one or two people who are close to you.

Meditating on God's Word

Read Jesus's final dialogue with his disciples in John 14:1–17:26, paying special attention to the relationship between the Father, Son, and Holy Spirit. Make note of the relationship of believers with each of them.

ANOINTING

But you have an anointing from the Holy One,
and all of you know the truth.

1 John 2:20 (NIV)

There are many references in the Bible to someone being anointed with olive oil. Now, as in ancient times, olives are very important in the Middle East, both as a food and as a cash crop. Their abundance has long been a symbol of wealth and prosperity (Deut. 6:11; Hag. 2:19). Olive oil is very useful in cooking (1 Kings 17:12–16)—did you ever try to turn a cake out of a pan you forgot to grease? It is also used in medicine (Mark 6:13; James 5:14) and in lotions and perfumes, both for daily grooming (Ezek. 16:9; Matt. 6:17–18) and for special occasions (Ruth 3:3; Luke 7:46). No wonder it is associated with joy and blessing (Deut. 7:13; Ps. 23:5). It was burned for light (Exod. 27:20; Matt. 25:1–10), used as payment (2 Chron. 2:10; Hosea 2:5; Ezra 3:7), and was often a part of religious offerings (Exod. 29:39–40; Num. 6:15).

The practice of anointing is no longer familiar to us except in some religious settings. (Anointing is sometimes called "unction" from the Latin term *unctio* or "chrism" from the Greek *chrisma*.) In the Old Testament, a ceremony that included pouring olive oil over one's head was used to mark someone chosen by God and set apart for his service. Prophets, priests, and kings were all anointed. The anointing of a new king was often accompanied by political drama. Solomon was chosen by David instead of his older brother Adonijah (1 Kings 1), and the prophet who anointed Jehu in private fled immediately afterward (2 Kings 9:1–14). For the anointing of Aaron and his sons when they were ordained as priests (Exod. 40:12–15), a special blend of spices and olive oil was prepared, which was only to be used in temple ceremonies (Exod. 30:22–33). God directed that the prophet Elisha be anointed as Elijah's successor (1 Kings 19:16; see also Isa. 61:1 for the anointing of a prophet).

The oil symbolized God's blessing and the presence of his Spirit with the one being anointed. "Then Samuel took the horn of oil, and anointed him in the midst of his brothers; and the Spirit of the LORD came mightily upon David from that day forward" (1 Sam. 16:13 RSV). To refer to someone as "the Lord's anointed" recognized that person's special position (Ps. 105:15). It also indicated the folly of interfering with the anointed one or his work—after David was anointed he still would not harm Saul (1 Sam. 24:6–7, 10; 26:9–11, 23–24), because Saul had been anointed king before him.

The Hebrew word "Messiah" and the Greek word "Christ" both mean "anointed one." The heart of early Christian preaching is that Jesus is the Christ, the anointed one of God. In the first gospel sermon, Peter proclaimed, "God has made this Jesus, whom you crucified, both Lord and Christ" (Acts 2:36 NIV). Jesus was the fulfillment of Old Testament prophecy, and this was confirmed by his resurrection (Acts 2:30–33). To deny that Jesus is the Christ, the Son of God, is a lie, which excludes one from enjoying eternal life (1 John 2:23–25).

As the Messiah, Jesus is prophet (Luke 13:33; 24:19–20) and yet more than a prophet—a Son (Heb. 1:1–3). Jesus is our priest (Heb. 5:6–10) and yet more than even a high priest—he is himself the sinless sacrifice (Heb. 7:24–27). Jesus Christ is king (John 18:33–37) and yet more than king—he will reign eternally over all creation (1 Cor. 15:24–26; Rev. 19:16).

In Hebrew and in Latin the word for anointing refers to the act of anointing someone, as does the Greek word *chrisis*. But Greek also has another word for anointing: *chrisma*, which refers instead to the olive oil (or other substance) used in the ceremony. Both Greek words were used for *anointing* both before and after New Testament times, but it is the word *chrisma* that is used for *anointing* in the New Testament, and it is from this word that the English term "chrism" comes. The emphasis for *chrisma* is not what is done, but the substance with which one is anointed. This means that when 1 John 2:20–27 speaks of the church as being anointed with the Holy Spirit, the emphasis is not on the act of anointing but on the Holy Spirit which remains present in the church. The word *chrisma* became the usual word for anointing in early Christian writings, perhaps because of the importance of the Holy Spirit.

In the early church, and in some traditions today, anointing with oil was a part of the baptismal ceremony by which one becomes a Christian. The oil symbolizes the presence of the

Holy Spirit. (The New Testament does not mention oil as part of a baptismal ceremony, but does connect the Holy Spirit with baptism.) It reminds us that the Spirit is at work in conversion and only through the Spirit can there be unity in the church. Just as the Spirit descended on Christ at his baptism (Matt. 3:16–17), so also when Christians are baptized they "receive the gift of the Holy Spirit" (Acts 2:38 NIV).

In 1 John there are two safeguards against those who would deceive Christians. If apostolic teaching (2:24) and "the anointing" (2:27) abide in believers, then the believers will abide in the Son and in the Father. In this passage, "the anointing" would not refer to olive oil, but to the presence of the Holy Spirit. Those who have been "anointed by the Holy One" (2:20 RSV) are also taught by that anointing (2:27), and so are able to discern truth from lies and not be misled by teachers who do not speak the truth. It is the teaching of the apostles and the presence of the Holy Spirit that protect believers.

In Old Testament times, prophets, priests, and kings were all anointed in a special ceremony that set them apart for a particular service to God. Jesus is *the* anointed one, the Messiah, the Christ. His role as God's Son and as Savior is unique. A person who is baptized into Christ participates in his anointing. Thus, Christians are set apart to do God's will and are able to do this because of the Holy Spirit.

Questions and Reflection

What has been your experience with literal anointing with oil as a religious practice?

What contemporary marks of favor or designations of leadership are used today in similar ways to anointing in the ancient world?

First John 2:27 says "the anointing" (*chrisma*) teaches Christians so they will not be deceived. What are some of the ways the Holy Spirit guides in discerning what is true teaching from God? Use the following passages:

2 Timothy 3:16–17	1 Kings 3:9–12
Hebrews 5:14	James 3:14–17

What are your favorite songs about the Holy Spirit or the work of the Spirit in Christians?

Look up the verses in the first column to see some of the things priests do. The passages in the second column show Jesus in one of these priestly roles. 1 Peter 2:9 describes the church as "a royal priesthood." The third column has passages illustrating similar Christian responsibilities.

Deuteronomy 31:9, 11	John 7:14–16	Colossians 3:16
Exodus 40:12–15	Mark 9:2–7	Colossians 3:12–14
2 Chronicles 30:27	Luke 5:16	Ephesians 6:18
Deuteronomy 21:5	John 5:30	1 Corinthians 6:3–6
Leviticus 1:10–13	Hebrews 2:17	Romans 12:1

Psalm 133:2 (RSV) describes a blessing as "like the precious oil upon the head, running down upon the beard, upon the beard of Aaron, running down on the collar of his robes!" My dad, however, says, "It doesn't sound so great to have olive oil running down your beard!!" How is being set apart for service to God a blessing? In what ways might it not always feel like a blessing?

Prayer
Read 1 Peter 2:4-10 and give thanks
for Christ, the Messiah.

Meditating on God's Word

Read Leviticus 20:22–22:16 for some of the rules for priests to be ceremonially "clean" and for some of the special restrictions put on those anointed as priests.

AREOPAGUS/
MARS' HILL

*So Paul, standing in the middle of the Areopagus,
said: "Men of Athens, . . ."*

Acts 17:22 (RSV)

*Then Paul stood in the midst of Mars' hill, and said,
Ye men of Athens, . . .*

Acts 17:22 (KJV)

If you go to Athens, you may be taken to a rocky hill near the Acropolis known as Mars' Hill, or the Areopagus. You will be told that is where Paul stood when he gave his famous speech recorded in Acts 17. A bronze plaque containing the Greek text of the speech is attached to the rock. In the 1611 King James Version, Acts 17:22 reads: "Then Paul stood in the midst of Mars' hill and said, Ye men of Athens, I perceive that in all things ye are too superstitious."

It would be difficult for Paul to stand in the middle of the solid rock of Mars' Hill. He could, however, stand in the middle of the meeting of the high court called the Areopagus.

In ancient times (long before Paul) the law court of Athens met on Mars' Hill (in a building that no longer exists). The word "Areopagus" comes from *Ares*, the Greek god of war, and *pagus*, a word for "hill." (Mars is the Roman god of war.) The Greek name for the hill is Areopagus, which means the Hill of Ares (or Mars for the Romans). The court of the Areopagus received its name from the place where it met in earlier times. Today, the high court in Athens is still called the Areopagus.

When Paul was in Athens, the Areopagus (high court) usually met in the Royal Stoa, a building in the marketplace (the Agora), which is located below the Acropolis. (It will likely also be pointed out on your tour of Athens.) At that time, the court would probably only have used the Hill of Mars or the Areopagus as the place from which to announce the death sentence of a condemned prisoner.

Today's English Version translates that verse as "Paul stood up in front of the meeting of the Areopagus." Paul's speech would have been made to the court, probably meeting in a building below Mars' Hill. He spoke boldly of the one true God to the leaders of a city that worshiped many gods. One of the members of that court—a man named Dionysius—was among the first believers in Athens.

Questions and Reflection

Read Acts 17:22–31. What would you say is the main theme of Paul's speech?

Paul usually quotes Old Testament passages in his sermons (Acts 13:16–47, at the synagogue in Antioch of Pisidia, has at least half a dozen quotations) and letters (Galatians has twelve, Ephesians has five, and many more in Romans and in the Corinthian letters), but there are no Old Testament quotes in this speech before the Athenian court. Why do you think that might be?

Look up the word "Athens" in a concordance and read other passages in the New Testament to see what Paul says elsewhere about what was on his mind while he was in Athens.

What public occasions are there for sharing faith today?

What are your favorite evangelistic songs or hymns?

One of the themes in the book of Acts is the conversion of prominent people to the gospel. Read the following verses and note who responded to the gospel in each:

Acts 8:27, 38	Acts 16:14–15
Acts 9:1–3, 17–18	Acts 16:27–34
Acts 10:1–2, 48	Acts 17:1–4, 10–12
Acts 13:7, 12	Acts 18:8

Where do Christians and Christianity fit in society today?

Influential?   Persecuted?

Marginal?   Persecuting?

How (if at all) does your evaluation of Christianity's current status in society change how you interact with culture?

Do you feel the need to behave differently if you are part of a persecuted minority than if you are part of a dominant influence?

Prayer

Read Romans 10:14–17 and say a prayer for all those who have not heard the gospel—especially for those in your own community who may never have heard it. Read Ephesians 6:18–20, and pray for those who have received the gospel.

Meditating on God's Word

Compare Peter's speech to the Jews gathered for the Pentecost festival in Jerusalem shortly after Jesus's crucifixion in Acts 2:14–36 to his speech to the family and friends of the Roman centurion Cornelius in Acts 10:34–43. What differences do you see in the themes and content of the two speeches? What elements do both have in common?

ASSEMBLY

When they came to Jerusalem, they were welcomed by
the church *and the apostles and elders, to whom they*
reported everything God had done through them.

Acts 15:4 (NIV—italics added)

What is the church? What should be done in church? These are two very important questions that may be answered from the Bible. The Greek word usually translated as "church" is *ekklesia*, and it is the word for "assembly."

This word can be used for any kind of gathering. It is used three times in connection with a riot in Ephesus. In Acts 19:39 (RSV), after calming the rioters, the town clerk urged them to settle things "in the regular assembly" (obviously not referring to an assembly of the Lord's church because preaching the gospel was the reason for the riot!). The word *ekklesia* is also used for the rowdy gathering itself (Acts 19:32, 41). There are many kinds of assemblies and reasons for assembling, and *ekklesia* could be used for any of them; the emphasis of the word is on coming together for a common purpose.

This Greek word for assembly, or church, is used in Acts 7:38 in Stephen's speech before he was stoned, in which he refers to the "assembly in the wilderness" (NIV). Here, he means the company of Israelites who were wandering in the wilderness, not the church described elsewhere in the New Testament. The church is people gathered by God "those sanctified in Christ Jesus . . . who in every place call on the name of our Lord Jesus Christ . . ." (1 Cor. 1:2 RSV). When the whole church comes together as a church, Christians call on the name of the Lord; that is, they assemble to worship him. There are several passages in 1 Corinthians where Paul makes distinctions between what is done "in church" and what is done "at home" (11:20–22, 33–34; 14:34–35). In the early centuries, the church met in the homes of its members, so the distinction is not a matter of location; the activities and purposes of home and church are quite different. Not every meeting of Christians is an assembly of the church: a Christian family and their dinner guests may pray together, but this is "home" not "church"; a gathering for Bible study at home or at the church building may be a "church activity" yet does not have to be the "church assembly."

The importance of the Christian assembly is also seen not only in the instructions given for it, but also in the variety of terms used for it in the New Testament: "come together" (1 Cor. 11:17, 20, 33–34; 14:26 *sunerchetai*), "gather together" (Acts 20:7–8; Heb. 10:25 *sunagogein* [from which the word "synagogue" derives]), and "in the same place" (Acts 2:44; 1 Cor. 11:20; 14:23 *epi to auto*) to mention a few. (This variety of terms also makes it easy to overlook the assembly context of some passages until a closer study is done.)

Among the purposes of the Christian assembly are to glorify God (Eph. 3:21), to exemplify the church (1 Cor. 11:18; 14:33), to edify Christians (1 Cor. 14:26), to encourage fellowship (Acts 2:42, 46; Heb. 10:24–25), and to commemorate and proclaim salvation (1 Cor. 10:16–17, 11:23–26). Although the rare mention of when the New Testament church came together as the church in Acts 20:7 seems almost incidental, it is no accident that the church met to commemorate the Lord's death (Luke 22:19; 1 Cor. 11:23–26) on the first day of the week—the day of his resurrection (Matt. 28:1; Mark 16:1–2; Luke 24:1, 13; John 20:1). Sunday, the day of the Christian assembly, came to be referred to as "the Lord's day" (Rev. 1:10).

Activities in the assembly occasionally include confession of faith (1 Tim. 6:12), missionary reports (Acts 14:27), selecting and appointing leaders (Acts 6:2, 5–6), and exercising discipline (1 Cor. 5:4–5). Activities normally in the assembly include:

1. The Lord's Supper (Acts 20:7; 1 Cor. 11:20–33); also called thanksgiving (or "Eucharist" Matt. 26:27), communion (1 Cor. 10:16–17), breaking of bread (Acts 20:7)
2. Prayer (1 Cor. 14:14–16)
3. Singing (1 Cor. 14:15–16, 26)
4. Giving (1 Cor. 16:1–2)
5. Reading and preaching the Bible (1 Tim. 4:13, 1 Cor. 14:19, 26)

Hebrews 10:25 hints at the importance of Christians assembling together when urging readers not to stop coming together. God knew that Christians would need each other, and so he made plans from the beginning for his church—his assembly.

> ". . . to make plain to everyone the administration of
> this mystery, which for ages past was kept hidden in
> God, who created all things. His intent was that now,
> through the church, the manifold wisdom of God
> should be made known to the rulers and authori-
> ties in the heavenly realms, according to his eternal
> purpose which he accomplished in Christ Jesus our
> Lord." (Eph. 3:9–11 NIV)

Actually, if the church does not assemble on a regular basis, it
will cease to be a church—by definition and in practice. Several
years ago, I read an article reporting on two different missionary groups and their experiences, working in the same
general area. One group taught about Jesus and emphasized
the importance of church attendance. The other group taught
about Jesus, but did not teach about the church. The leaders of
both groups eventually moved away. Several years later someone came to the same area looking for Christians. Of the group
that did not teach about the church, none could be found.
However, of the group that had been taught about the church,
there was a thriving group of Christians who continued to
assemble weekly in church. This illustrates the importance of
the assembly and God's wisdom in planning for his church
from the beginning.

The "church" is the assembly of God's people. It refers both
to the people themselves and to their meeting together as an
expression of their identity in Christ. When the church meets
together, they worship according to his purposes and desires;
they celebrate and proclaim salvation, and they edify one
another, all to the glory of God. The activities in the assembly

are done because of love for God and a desire to please him. These include partaking of the Lord's Supper; prayer and the singing of hymns; giving, reading, and preaching the Word of God; and sometimes the exercise of church discipline, appointment of leaders, hearing messages from other churches, or confessions of faith. Whether in the assembly or not, Christians are the church, a new people created in Christ to do good works (Eph. 2:10) and to glorify God.

---

* We are indebted to Everett Ferguson, chapter 4, "Worship and Assembly," in *The Church of Christ: A Biblical Ecclesiology for Today* (Grand Rapids: Eerdmans, 1997), especially pp. 231–233 for terms and pp. 243–256 for the purposes of and activities in church.

Questions and Reflection

Consider your experience in church assemblies.

How do you feel about attending church?

What practical benefits have you obtained from church involvement?

What spiritual benefits have you received through the assembly?

Which of these benefits is the result of being part of a community of believers, and which is the direct result of meeting together regularly as the church?

Which of the benefits of meeting together might properly be described as the purpose of the church's meeting together, and which are more likely by-products of assembling for other purposes?

In Greek, the following verses have the word *ekklesia*, which is usually translated "church." Look up the first three and consider what difference it might it make in your understanding of what the early church was like if you substitute "assembly" for "church."

Acts 5:11	Acts 9:31	Acts 12:1, 5	Acts 14:23, 27
Acts 8:3	Acts 11:26	Acts 13:1	Acts 16:5

How would you explain to a friend who knows very little about church what your church does when it comes together?

Look up the word "church" in a dictionary to see how it developed from a Greek word (*kuriakos*) meaning "belonging to the Lord." This word is used only twice in the New Testament: 1 Corinthians 11:20 and Revelation 1:10. Turn to these passages to see what is designated as belonging to the Lord.

Consider the words of the hymn "The Church's One Foundation" and how it reflects the concept of the church as people called together by God for a common purpose.

Prayer

Take from Hebrews 10:23-27 three things that you can pray for your church. Pause for a moment to pray for these things now.

Meditating on God's Word

Consider these aspects of the Lord's Supper and the Old Testament background:

memorial meal (remembering Christ's atoning sacrifice), 1 Corinthians 11:24-26; compare to the Passover, Exodus 12; Leviticus 2:9-10

covenant feast (celebrating a relationship), Mark 14:23-24; compare Genesis 31:51-55; Exodus 24:7-11

messianic banquet (anticipating the future), Matthew 26:29, Revelation 19:9; compare Isaiah 25:6-9

ATONING SACRIFICE

*He is the atoning sacrifice for our sins, and not only for
ours but also for the sins of the whole world.*

1 John 2:2 (NIV)

To sacrifice usually means giving up something of value
in order to gain something else. It used to refer to a religious offering, especially to an animal killed ceremonially. To
atone means to make amends for wrong that has been done.
Scripture speaks of Christ and his death as an "atoning sacrifice." Christ willingly gave himself to die in our place. His sacrifice made it possible for God to reconcile humans to himself
(2 Cor. 5:20–21). He atoned for our sins; that is, he provided
the way for man to become one ("at-one") with God.

"Atoning sacrifice" (NIV, NRSV, NET), "propitiation" (ASV,
KJV, NASB, ESV), and "expiation" (RSV) are all translations of
the same Greek word, and they all refer to ways to achieve forgiveness of sins. Yet there are slight differences in the meaning
of the English words used to translate the Greek.

"Propitiation" usually carries with it the idea of appeasement. In pagan worship, the worshipper thought that if he gave the gods a good enough sacrifice, then the gods would be happy with him and would bless him. It was a matter of barter: "I'll give you a nice sacrifice if you give me what I want." Propitiation usually has as its object a person, or being. It is done to put someone (persons or gods) in a good mood, willing to grant the requests of the worshipper; it is done to appease them in order to achieve reconciliation.

"Expiation" carries with it the idea of erasing or extinguishing a wrong; making amends for something. Expiation is done to correct a situation—to erase a misdeed. It usually refers to what is done to correct one's own mistakes and make things right.

The main distinction between the two English words is that propitiation is directed toward a person and expiation toward a thing (an error or a bad situation). Both ideas are present in all forms of the Greek word these terms translate, but most translators pick one or the other to use every time a form of the Greek term occurs.

The Greek noun *hilasmos* (propitiation/expiation) is used in 1 John 2:2 and 1 John 4:10. The related noun *hilasterion* (means or place of propitiation/expiation) is in Romans 3:25 (also in Hebrews 9:5, where it refers to the "Mercy Seat" over the Ark of the Covenant). The verb *hilaskesthai* (to make propitiation/expiation) is used in Hebrews 2:17 (and in Luke 18:13, where it is usually translated "be merciful").

"Atoning sacrifice" is a simpler term than either "propitiation" or "expiation," but it can carry both meanings: reconciliation and extinguishing wrongs.

Perhaps the pagan gods needed to be appeased with offerings, but the Almighty God, our heavenly Father, does not need what is offered to lifeless idols. Rather, he wants to reconcile us to himself and he wants us to love him from our hearts, obeying him in everything (1 Sam. 15:22; Rom. 12:1) because we love him and want to show him our love.

What is most amazing about the New Testament uses of this word is that they do not refer to sacrifices we offer to God to appease him and erase our sins, but to the sacrifice he provided to extinguish our sins and bring about reconciliation. Christ's sacrifice on the cross makes possible for us, who are all sinners and separated from God, to be made at one with him. When we obey God's plans for us and repent, our sins are erased, extinguished, and washed away in the waters of baptism (Acts 22:16).

The "atoning sacrifice" in these passages does not refer to anything we do to appease God or make amends for our own mistakes. It is God providing the means of erasing human error and reconciling sinners to himself.

Questions and Reflection

The Old Testament has many references to pagan sacrifices. In the verses below, who offered what to which god, and what was the desired result of that offering?

Numbers 25:1–3   2 Chronicles 24:7
1 Kings 11:4–6   Jeremiah 44:15–19
2 Kings 17:14–17   Hosea 4:12–13

These passages describe some of the sacrifices under the Law of Moses. What was the purpose of these sacrifices? What restrictions were there regarding when, how, and by whom they were done? What was the expected result of doing (or not doing) what was commanded?

Leviticus 17:10–12   Numbers 5:6–7
Leviticus 19:5–7   Deuteronomy 12:13–14
Leviticus 22:20–23   Ezekiel 43:25–27

Read the following passages and explain in your own words why Christ died, and what was accomplished by his death.

Hebrews 9:22   Romans 6:22–23   1 Peter 1:18–21

From these passages, make a list of some ways Christians now offer sacrifices to God.

Psalm 69:30–31   2 Corinthians 9:1–2
Matthew 9:13   Philippians 4:18
Mark 12:33   Hebrews 13:15–16
Romans 12:1   Revelation 5:8

What hymns do you know that mention these types of sacrifices?

Look at the following passages written against those who were offering the required sacrifices, and yet were not pleasing to God. What seems to have been the problem?

Isaiah 1:11–17   Amos 5:21–24

In what ways might some of these problems still be trouble to us today?

Prayer

Read Hebrews 10:11–18 and offer a prayer of praise and thanksgiving for Christ and his sacrifice for sins.

Meditating on God's Word

Read Leviticus 5:1–6:7 on sin offerings. Use a study Bible and check some of the cross-references. Consider what this passage tells us about what is sinful, the seriousness of sin, and how we should respond when we recognize sin.

CUP

My cup runneth over.

Psalm 23:5 (KJV, ASV)

The Twenty-Third Psalm is a favorite of many. It describes the love of God for us as that of a good shepherd caring for his own sheep. Most of the psalm describes the work of a shepherd in terms that even those of us who never spent any time around sheep can understand: the shepherd makes sure the sheep can graze in good pastures and have plenty of water to drink; the shepherd protects his sheep and does everything he can to take good care of them. However, it may not be obvious what an overflowing cup would mean to sheep.

A look at one of the ancient water wells in Israel may help us understand. In Dothan, there is a well called Joseph's Well. It has large, round, cuplike depressions at the corners on each side. When we visited the site, our guide explained the purpose of these depressions (or cups). When the shepherd, or camel herder, led his thirsty animals to the well, the animals could not drink directly from the well, so the shepherd would draw water from the well and pour it into one of the cups. These depressions were too small for all the animals to drink from the same one, so the shepherd would continue drawing water and pouring it into the cuplike depression until the water ran over the edge and into a trough connecting the cups. Only when the overflowing water from the cup filled the trough would all the animals be able to drink.

Knowing something about the cultural context helps us to understand many passages of Scripture. Many things about the rural, agriculturally based lifestyle that is the background of much of the Bible are very different from the lifestyle of those who read it today, although people and their needs remain the same. Archaeology often helps us to understand that different world a little better, so that things written long ago come to life for us, and the message of Scripture becomes clearer.

In the Twenty-Third Psalm we see the comparison between the shepherd's careful attention to the needs of all his sheep and God's loving care for his children. Just as the water overflowed the cup beside the well and provided more than enough water for all the sheep to drink, so is God's love for us even more abundant than our needs require. God gives me everything I need for life and godliness (2 Pet. 1:3), and the Holy Spirit helps in my weakness (Rom. 8:26).

As Jesus rested by Jacob's well (near Sychar on the way from Jerusalem to Galilee), he said, "Every one who drinks of this water will thirst again, but whoever drinks of the water that I shall give him will never thirst; the water that I shall give him will become in him a spring of water welling up to eternal life"

WORDS TO LIVE BY

(John 4:13–14 RSV). God's provision for the spiritual needs of his followers is so abundant that it overflows from one person to another. We often receive help and encouragement from others, and yet God is the one on whom we rely to provide that help. When we are open to the leading of the Holy Spirit, we find that we can say with the psalmist, "My cup runneth over."

Questions and Reflection

Isaiah 44:3–4 makes a connection between water and the Spirit. Use an online concordance program to search for places in the New Testament where the words "water" and "spirit" occur together.

One reason sometimes given for coming to church each week is to "refill your cup" or to "recharge your batteries."

1. What is good about this picture?

2. What is wrong with it?

3. Should getting your cup filled be the purpose of assembly or its result?

Are you familiar with any of the melodies used to sing the Twenty-Third Psalm?

Read Ezekiel 34:11–19 and list five things that God does as shepherd of his people.

In John 10:1–18 Jesus describes himself as the Good Shepherd. From this passage list three things that make Jesus a good shepherd.

What are some of the ways God fills our spiritual cups with living water?

Prayer

Use the instructions in 1 Peter 5:1–4 to pray for the elders/shepherds who lead the church where you worship.

Meditating on God's Word

Read the eighth chapter of Romans and meditate on the role the Holy Spirit plays in a Christian's life.

DEACON

To all the saints in Christ Jesus who are at Philippi,
with the bishops and **deacons** ...
Philippians 1:1 (RSV—italics added)

If you put these instructions before the brethren,
you will be a good **minister** *of Christ Jesus.*
1 Timothy 4:6 (RSV—italics added)

His mother said to the **servants,** *"Do whatever he tells you."*
John 2:5 (RSV—italics added)

The Greek word, *diakonos*, can be translated by three different English words: "servant," "minister," or "deacon." Each English word has a slightly different meaning. We need to understand each of these words in order to see which one best gives the meaning of a particular passage.

The most common translation is "servant." It refers to a person who has been given a task. That task may be large or small. For instance, a person may be in charge of the household accounts of his employer. He has a task to perform for the owner of the house. There is no dishonor in being a servant. Indeed, some servants carry great responsibility, and there is always honor in doing one's work well.

There is another Greek word, *doulos,* which is sometimes translated "servant." It refers to a slave who belongs to another person. When Paul and other disciples describe themselves as slaves of Christ (Rom. 1:1, Phil. 1:1, Titus 1:1, etc.) they mean they totally belong to our Savior and are devoted to obeying him. At other times, they are called servants, *diakonos,* with the emphasis on work they do for Christ (1 Cor. 3:5–6, 2 Cor. 6:4, Eph. 3:7–8, etc.).

The second word used to translate *diakonos* is "minister." However, if we think only of the modern meaning of the word instead of thinking about what it meant when it was used in the New Testament we will get the wrong impression. We usually think of a minister as the preacher or pastor leading the congregation and we see it as a position of authority. Or perhaps we think of the powerful office of prime minister in some countries. But to minister means to be a servant. Many of the less celebrated ways of ministering, such as visiting the ill, comforting the grieving, caring for the elderly, and so on, come closer to the New Testament meaning of the word "minister," which was something more like a nurse ministering to patients (Col. 1:7, Heb. 1:14, etc.).

There are other Greek words that are sometimes also translated "minister." The term *leitourgos* is used for a priest, or one who performs religious duties (Rom. 15:16), and *huperetes* is used for an assistant who acts on behalf of one in authority (Acts 13:5). However, the word most often used in the New Testament for a Christian minister is not one of these more respected terms, but just the simple word for a servant, *diakonos.* This means the emphasis is usually not on the religious nature of the service or on the authority with which it is done, but simply on the fact that it is done for the benefit of others.

The third word used for *diakonos* is "deacon." It is a transliteration of the Greek word—that is, the Greek word is spelled with English letters, making up a new word instead of translating the Greek word into English. (Other transliterated words include "baptism" and "hallelujah.") Often, one seeing the word "deacon" thinks immediately of the office of deacon, which can mean different things in different churches today. In the New Testament, the word *diakonos* was not limited to church usage, but is usually only transliterated as "deacon" when referring to a servant of the church.

The primary meaning of *diakonos* is one who has been given a job to do for someone else, and so it could be used in a general sense for anyone who worked on behalf of the church in some specific way. It also came to be used in a specialized sense for those appointed to do a certain task in the church. Deacons are included with elders as having a special role in the church (Phil. 1:1, 1 Tim. 3). In the New Testament, this word does not indicate an exalted office, but rather reflects Jesus's own attitude of humble service, which his followers are to imitate.

There were many kinds of servants (deacons) in the New Testament. Each had particular responsibilities to perform. The word *diakonos* is applied to a number of different people in the New Testament, not all of whom were Christians.

1. Servants at a feast (John 2:5)
2. Governing authority (Rom. 13:4)
3. Emissaries of Satan (2 Cor. 11:14–15)

4. Christians (John 12:26)
5. Evangelists (1 Tim. 4:6)
6. Specific Christians
    0. Phoebe (Rom. 16:1)
    a. Tychicus (Eph. 6:21)
    b. Epaphras (Col. 1:7)
    c. and others
1. Christ (Rom. 15:8)
2. Apostles (Matt. 20:26)

One who would be a servant of God may or may not be appointed or recognized by the church in any specialized way. The important thing is to minister as faithful servants in whatever work one is called to do. A servant works for the benefit of others.

Questions and Reflection

In each of the following passages, who is called a deacon? What is the specific task this person is to do? Does the word "deacon" here seem to be a general word for a servant or a specialized term referring to someone holding a church office? (You may have to read a few verses before or after the one given to get enough context to answer.)

John 12:26   Philippians 1:1b
Romans 16:1   Colossians 1:7
1 Corinthians 3:5   Colossians 4:7

Use a concordance to locate other references to Tychicus and see what you can learn about where he came from and the work he did with Paul.

Read the following passages where the Apostle Paul describes himself as a servant, and briefly restate what each passage says about the nature of Christian service.

2 Corinthians 6:4–10   Ephesians 3:6–9

Read 1 Timothy 3:8–13 for the characteristics of deacons in the church. What does each thing listed indicate about the kinds of things deacons might be expected to do?

What is the role of deacons in your church? What qualifications are required of them?

How does it compare with the role of elders in your church?

In what ways do you serve the church? Which of the servants listed above served in ways most similar to ways you serve or would like to serve the church?

Prayer

Read Matthew 20:20-28. Consider what it
means to devote oneself to serve as Jesus did.
Pray for those who serve in your church.

Meditating on God's Word

Read 1 Corinthians 12–14 and consider how different people
and different types of service come together in the church for
God's glory.

EDIFY

Let each of us please his neighbor for his good, to edify him.

Romans 15:2 (RSV)

Those familiar with the use of the word "edify" outside a Christian context probably understand that it means providing some intellectual or spiritual benefit, or improving one's character. Those who are less familiar with the term may understand it just as a vague reference to something being good or pleasant.

An English dictionary is very helpful here. The English word "edify" comes from the Latin word for building and is related to the word "edifice." An edifice is a strong or imposing building. The Greek word it sometimes translates also means building: the verb "to build" (Matt. 21:33; Luke 7:5) usually refers to the construction of a building; the noun can refer to a literal structure (Matt. 24:1 NASB, "the temple *building*") or a metaphorical one (1 Cor. 3:9, "you are . . . God's *building*"), and it is frequently used for the process of creating something more intangible yet valuable (2 Cor. 12:19 NIV, "everything we do, dear friends, is for your *strengthening*").

The image of constructing a strong building or edifice is sometimes used for the church: "You are fellow citizens with the saints and members of the household of God, *built* upon the foundation of the apostles and prophets, Christ Jesus himself being the cornerstone, in whom the whole *structure* is joined together and grows into a holy temple in the Lord" (Eph. 2:19–21 RSV). This makes the terms "edify" and "edification" especially meaningful ways to describe things that are done for the good of the church.

Just as we reserve the use of the word "edifice" for a solidly built, imposing building and would not use it of a poorly built shack or a temporary stage set, so also does "edification" refer to the process of providing education and strength that will endure. It does not apply to things that simply feel good or look good, but only to that which has lasting value.

Since several different words are sometimes used to translate the various forms of the Greek word for "edify," it would be helpful to use a concordance that indicates the Greek words used, not just the English words. Throughout this discussion, the English translations of the Greek word for "edify" are given in italics.

A closer look at two passages where the metaphor of building is used (Eph. 4:9–16 and 1 Cor. 14:1–40) illustrates what is edifying.

Ephesians 4 is one of the passages on differing spiritual gifts, which are given "for *building up* the body of Christ" (4:12 RSV). The very differences we often find discouraging may be caused by the Holy Spirit, who has given us different gifts to bind us together and strengthen us in Christ. No one has every gift, so we must rely on each other so that the church may become complete and Christlike. Getting past initial discouragement and learning to work together in ways that honor differences will strengthen the church. And "the whole body, . . . when each part is working properly, makes bodily growth and *upbuilds* itself in love" (4:16 RSV). Edification refers to the process of moving toward maturity and unity of faith. Speech is an important aspect of that process: "speaking the truth in love" (4:15 RSV) is necessary. It is also important to "let no evil talk come out of your mouths, but only such as is good for *edifying*, as fits the occasion, that it may impart grace to those who hear" (4:29 RSV).

First Corinthians 14 is one of the most detailed discussions of the church assembly, and some form of the word "edify" appears six times in this chapter. "When you come together . . . let all things be done for *edification*" (14:26 RSV). The purpose of preaching is for "*strengthening*, encouraging and comfort" (14:3 NIV). The discussion in 14:2–5 makes clear that knowledge and understanding are necessary parts of edification. Not only the preaching, but also prayers and singing (14:16–17) should have content that can be understood by the worshipers so that edification can take place. While this passage deals with problems associated with the Corinthians speaking in tongues, the principle has other applications. If the preaching is in a language you do not understand, you may feel good for having been present, but you will not be edified. If you cannot follow the words of the hymns, you may appreciate and even be excited by the beauty of the music, but you will not be edified. If the prayers are mumbled softly, you may still be touched by the emotion of the speaker, but you will not be edified. Edification requires understanding. Emotional uplift is temporary, but when edification takes place, the echoes of wisdom remain long after the feelings have changed. The mind and will are affected, leaving peace and the strength to cope with life's challenges. Edification is the education, strengthening, and maturing of the church. It happens because of the Holy Spirit (14:12).

The term "edify" may not be well understood, but it is a strong word, referring to the process of creating something of lasting value. To edify others does not mean merely to provide them with some temporary feeling of well-being. It means to strengthen them with the knowledge, skills, and faith needed to live godly lives in this fallen world. Edification is one of the purposes of the church assembly.

Questions and Reflection

The image of a building is one of many used for the church. What other images appear in the following passages, and what is the main point being made by the use of each image?

Matthew 20:1–2	1 Peter 4:17
1 Corinthians 12:12	Revelation 19:7–8

Luke 2:52 lists four types of growth: physical, intellectual, social, and spiritual. What things can contribute to strengthening an individual in each of these areas?

Physical   Social
Intellectual/Mental   Spiritual

Look up Titus 2:1 in several different translations. What different phrases are used to describe what should be taught? How does each reflect some aspect of what is necessary for edification to take place?

First Corinthians 14:26 says that everything done in the assembly should edify the church. Look at the following passages and explain how each activity in the assembly might provide edification.

1 Corinthians 2:4–5   Colossians 3:16
1 Corinthians 4:16–17   Colossians 4:16
1 Corinthians 11:23–26   1 Timothy 2:1–4

Speech plays an important role in edification. Read the following passages from Proverbs, and list some of the things words can do:

Proverbs 10:11, 17–21, 31–32; 12:6, 18, 25

Many songs sung in church make worshipers feel good. What are some songs that also edify mentally and spiritually?

Prayer

Read 1 Timothy 4:11–16 and pray for someone you know who is working to build up the church, either near you or in a mission field far away.

Meditating on God's Word

In 1 Thessalonians 5:11, Paul writes, "Therefore encourage one another and *build up* each other, as indeed you are doing" (NRSV). Read the entire letter (five chapters) and consider how both the teaching of the letter and the conduct encouraged serve to strengthen the church.

FAITH

And without faith it is impossible to please God.

Hebrews 11:6 (NIV)

We often hear that the biblical definition of faith is found in Hebrews 11:1, "the assurance of things hoped for, the conviction of things not seen" (RSV). However, in reality, most of that chapter is a description of what faith does, not what faith is. For example: faith helps us understand that God created the universe (Heb. 11:3); faith caused Abel to offer a better sacrifice than his brother (v. 4); faith allowed Enoch to be taken from this earth without experiencing death (v. 5). The rest of Hebrews 11 also tells things faith caused each person to do.

The best definition of biblical faith that I have found is in Romans 4:18–24. "Against all hope, Abraham in hope believed. . . . Yet he did not waver through unbelief regarding the promise of God, but was strengthened in his faith and gave glory to God, being fully persuaded that God had power to do what he had promised" (4:18, 20–21 NIV).

God had promised Abraham that he would be the father of a great nation (Gen. 12:1–3) but Abraham and Sarah had no children. Abraham was 75 years old, and Sarah was about 65 years old when the promise was first given (Gen. 12:4). From his knowledge of normal human reproduction, Abraham knew the difficulty involved in their having children. The promise was repeated twice after an interval of several years (Gen. 15:5; 17:5–8, 15–17). It was virtually impossible for Abraham and Sarah to have children at their ages. Yet Abraham still believed that God could and would keep his promise. In fact, Romans 4:21 says he was "fully convinced" (RSV); "fully persuaded" (NIV, KJV); "absolutely sure" (GNT); "absolutely convinced" (Phillips). This should give you an idea of how strong his faith was and provide an example to strengthen your own faith. By the time Isaac was born (Gen. 21:1–7), Abraham was about 100 years old, and Sarah was about 90 years old. Faith continues to believe God even when it seems impossible that his promises can be kept. But this is not unreasonable: God has a very good record of keeping promises.

The New Testament uses the word "faith" in at least three ways:

1. Jude uses the word in one way when he refers to "the faith," meaning the facts of the gospel. "I felt compelled to write and urge you to contend for the faith that was once for all entrusted to God's holy people." (Jude 3, NIV) "The faith" contains the facts of the gospel given to Christians. There is no other gospel,

although there are false teachers even today claiming that they have a different gospel. Jude urged the Christians to hold up the facts of the gospel—the death, burial, and resurrection of Jesus (1 Cor. 15:1–11); salvation in Christ (Gal. 3:10–14); and other important concepts they knew to be true.

2. A second aspect of faith is belief, which includes accepting as true the body of information presented in the Bible as the inspired Word of God. It involves comprehending that God exists; that is, giving intellectual agreement to what the Bible says. This second aspect of faith is believing that the gospel is true and that God exists, whether we act on our belief or not.

3. A third aspect of faith is trust. This is what faith most often means in Scripture. Intellectual acceptance of the facts revealed to us about God and what he has done for us throughout history is the first step in trusting Him: When we believe the things that the Bible says about God, we know that he is trustworthy. We know that he is willing and able to do what he has promised. This was the faith of Abraham. We can trust Him with our lives. And that is what we must do—turn our lives over to God so that we can live by faith.

Scripture sometimes uses the word "faith" in the first sense, meaning the content of what is believed. Having faith alone is not enough; it matters what one believes. Scripture only uses the word in the second sense, meaning intellectual acceptance, while pointing out that that is not saving faith—one's thinking and behavior should be changed by faith. The demons believe that God exists, but it does not do them any good because they do nothing except tremble at the thought (James 2:19). The vast majority of times the word "faith" appears in Scripture, it is in the third sense, meaning life-changing trust in God. God expects us to act on our faith (James 2:14–18).

Some people trust they will be saved simply because they have faith, but this is having faith in faith. Biblical faith, saving faith, is not about one's own feelings or attitudes, but is concerned with the object of that faith, God and his promises in Christ. It is believing the facts of the gospel and trusting our lives to Christ because of what he has done and what he will do. Trust depends on what is trusted, and the word "faith" in Scripture can refer to what is believed as well as to the act of believing.

Living by faith includes acting on our faith, obeying what God says, committing our lives to God, and expecting to go to heaven. This aspect of faith is trusting Jesus. It is a very important meaning of faith, and it builds on the other two meanings. One who has this kind of faith may be described as faithful, just as Abraham was.

Questions and Reflection

Look up the following passages and determine how "faith" is used in each. Is it used in the first sense—the content of the gospel—or is it used in the third sense—confidence and trust in God? (In some cases, either sense may fit.)

Acts 20:21   Philippians 1:27

Romans 1:12	Colossians 1:4
Romans 4:16	Colossians 2:7
1 Corinthians 2:5	2 Thessalonians 1:3
Galatians 1:23	1 Timothy 3:9
Ephesians 4:5	1 Timothy 5:8

Use an online concordance to look up "the faith" (exact phrase) in the book of Acts (RSV, NIV, or NKJV) and study each context to see what the term includes. Try rephrasing the verse to preserve the meaning without using the word "faith."

How do you feel when hearing about great heroes of the faith or when reading of Abraham's incredible faith?

Some people find that when they read Hebrews 11 and other such passages (taking them to heart) they feel discouraged. And yet Romans 15:4 says: "whatever was written in former days was written for our instruction, that by steadfastness and by the encouragement of the scriptures we might have hope" (RSV). What might need to change in one's thinking or way of reading Scripture for these passages to bring the encouragement and hope intended?

Romans 4:20–21 speaks of Abraham's unwavering faith in God's promise that he and Sarah would have many descendants, and yet Genesis 16 tells of his having a child by Hagar and Genesis 17:17 tells how he laughed at the idea of having a son with Sarah at their age. How do you explain/understand Abraham's faith in a way that allows for these apparent indications of lack of faith?

Prayer

Read Hebrews 11:21–31 making a list of what faith caused each person to do, or how faith changed that person. Pray for faith like theirs.

Meditating on God's Word

Read the letter to the Galatians, paying special attention to the themes of "faith" and "gospel."

FELLOWSHIP

Our fellowship is with the Father,
and with his Son Jesus Christ.

1 John 1:3 (KJV)

I n most churches, to "have fellowship" means to socialize—usually at a potluck (or pitch-in) dinner or other event involving food. Many church buildings even have a "fellowship hall" adjoining the church kitchen for this purpose. While eating and socializing together can be an important church activity, this is not the sum of what is meant by "fellowship" in the New Testament.

Because "fellowship" is usually a Christian word, the term is not often used for the fellowship of people who have shared an experience (such as a vacation, work in the same profession, or time in a combat zone) or who have certain traits, values, or interests in common. These other situations often describe a significant fellowship whose meaning may be closer to the meaning of the term in the New Testament.

The Greek word for fellowship is *koinonia*. Its basic meaning is a partnership. (This is usually what it meant in papyri and inscriptions from New Testament times.) Luke 5:10 uses it for a business partnership. Fellowship means cooperation or joint participation in some endeavor.

Scripture speaks of Christians having been called by God into fellowship (partnership) with Jesus Christ (1 Cor. 1:9) and having fellowship (being partners with) the Holy Spirit (2 Cor. 13:14). To have fellowship with Christ is to be a partner in his work of redemption. This is expressed in several ways in the New Testament.

Contribution of Material Goods

The most common use of the word *koinonia* ("fellowship") in the New Testament is in reference to financial gifts given by Christians to help other Christians in poverty or times of famine (2 Cor. 8:4; 9:13; Rom. 12:13; 15:26; Heb. 13:16). Giving financially should always be considered as fellowship. When we give money to a charity, we participate in all the good works the organization does. (Unfortunately, we also may become unwitting partners in misdeeds of the organization.) In the New Testament, Christians always entrusted such gifts to other Christians who had proven their ability to handle fiduciary responsibility faithfully (1 Cor. 16:3; 2 Cor. 8:18–21), and reports on the distribution of funds were expected (as is customary whenever someone handles funds for others, and as seen in Jesus's parables in Luke 16:2 and Matt. 25:19).

Cooperation in Advancement of the Gospel

One may have fellowship ("share," 1 Cor. 9:23 and Gal. 6:6) in the advancement of the gospel both by one's own actions as teacher and example, and also by the help and blessings one gives to others who are directly engaged in evangelism. To contribute financially to one who is teaching and living out the gospel in another culture is to have fellowship with them in the advancement of the gospel. (This is not the same thing as participating in good works. For example, to help provide a village with clean water or support an orphanage may be expressions of faith, but they do not necessarily involve proclaiming the gospel.) Fellowship with others who are proclaiming the gospel may involve financial support, regular prayers on their behalf (Col. 4:12), gifts and letters of encouragement to them and their families (Phil. 2:25; 4:10–18), or other forms of support.

Sharing in the Sufferings of Christ

The word *koinonia* is sometimes used in connection with suffering (Phil. 3:10–11; 1 Pet. 4:13). We would rather avoid suffering than embrace it. Theology that emphasizes the blessings found in Christ is, of course, much more popular than a theology of suffering, but Scripture contains both. Christ, in becoming human, accepted all the suffering that is part of human existence. It is by his suffering and death that he saved us, and we should expect some (temporary) suffering because of our faith (John 16:33). Christians, in imitation of Christ, rejoice to share his sufferings (Acts 5:40–41) and look for opportunities to show mercy to those who are suffering (Luke 6:36).

Common Life

We may enjoy our common life in Christ (Acts 2:42) by eating together with other Christians and enjoying other activities with one another. However, there is much more to fellowship than going to the ball game or shopping together—we can do that with others who are not Christians and may have at least as much fun. The common life in Christ also involves devotion to Bible study, time spent together in prayer, and regular participation in weekly assembly to take the Lord's Supper.

Our common interests may provide opportunities for participation with others—both Christians and non-Christians. Sometimes these are opportunities for evangelism or strengthening our faith and building relationships with other Christians, but it would be a mistake to assume that we are enjoying Christian fellowship every time we do something together with friends who happen to be Christians: if Christ is not at the center of our relationship and the activity it may be a different sort of fellowship. Philippians 2:1 and 4 says, "if you have . . . any common sharing in the Spirit . . . [look not] to your own interests but each of you to the interests of the others" (NIV). It is assumed that everyone will have different interests and concerns. It is only through the Holy Spirit that some Christians have anything in common with one another. We are more comfortable with people who are more like us, but it is time spent with Christians who share little except salvation in Christ that is most clearly Christian fellowship.

Agreement in Doing the Lord's Work

Koinonia is used in cooperation in the Lord's work (Gal. 2:9). Christians come from different backgrounds, have differing perspectives, and diverse gifts. Unity in Christ does not require uniformity. It does require respect for one another and acknowledgement of the fact that the work of the Holy Spirit may look very different in one life than it does in another (Gal. 5:25–26).

The hand and the eye need each other (1 Cor. 12:14–26); in Christ, the gift of teaching and the gift of mercy can complement each other rather than clashing. Christians who see things differently may use different methods while still respecting one another and the work the other is doing for Christ. They may work side by side for a common goal (as Paul did with Aquila and Priscilla in Acts 18:1–4) or they may work separately (as did Paul and John Mark for a time—Acts 15:36–41; see also 2 Tim. 4:11) with limited contact while still being in fellowship with one another.

Note on Disfellowship

The withdrawal of fellowship (or excommunication) is rarely practiced today, and is not always respected as New Testament teaching by those who have heard of it. Perhaps this is because on those rare occasions when it has been attempted it has often not been done in the right way.

Withdrawal of fellowship from those who are immoral (1 Cor. 5:11) or who cause division in the church (Titus 3:10–11) is intended to protect the church from sin (1 Cor. 5:5–7), to bring the sinner to repentance (2 Thess. 3:14–15), and to preserve the reputation of the church (Col. 4:5). It should be done in a spirit of love and patience (Matt. 18:15–17; Titus 3:9–10), and with respect for the Lord (1 Cor. 4:1–5).

When Christians celebrate fellowship that has the depth and breadth described above (and in Acts 2:45–47), the loss of contact involved in withdrawal of fellowship (1 Cor. 5:11; 2 Thess. 3:6; 2 John 10–11) has a significant impact and provides an opportunity for the positive changes intended by biblical teaching.

Summary

We have fellowship with Christ when we work together with other Christians to accomplish his purposes (not our own); when we enjoy a common life of faith (prayer and hope) with other Christians (whether or not they have anything but faith in common with us); when we participate in the suffering of Christ; when we cooperate in the advancement of the gospel; and when we contribute financially to the needs of other Christians.

Questions and Reflection

What do the following verses say about the basis of Christian fellowship?

Romans 12:4–5	Ephesians 4:4–6
2 Corinthians 1:21–22	2 Corinthians 5:17–18
Galatians 3:26–29	1 John 1:1–3
Romans 6:7–11	1 Corinthians 1:30

Romans 8:14–17 describes God as an adoptive father. Do you know anyone who has adopted a child from another

country, or several children born into different families? What are some of the challenges they have faced in creating a new family, and how do these correspond to the challenges faced in the church when members come from very different backgrounds?

Read 1 Corinthians 16:1–3 for Paul's instructions to the (Gentile) church at Corinth regarding the collection for famine relief for (Jewish) churches in Judea:

How was each person to determine how much to give?

When was it to be gathered in a common place ready for Paul's coming?

What reason was given for collecting small amounts over time?

How would the funds be delivered to Jerusalem?

What effect (other than practical) might this collection be expected to have, particularly on the relationship between Jewish and Gentile churches?

2 Corinthians 8:16–23 talks about those who are handling relief funds.

How many different people are mentioned?

What are some of the characteristics of the men chosen for this work?

What is Paul's goal (verses 20–21) in the way money is handled?

What do the following passages say about the spiritual significance of material gifts?

Romans 15:26–27   2 Corinthians 9:11–15
2 Corinthians 8:3–7   Hebrews 13:16

The word *koinonia* appears three times in the letter to the Philippians: 1:5, *koinonia* in the gospel; 2:1, spiritual *koinonia*; 3:10, *koinonia* in his sufferings. Look at these verses in your favorite Bible version and see how they are translated. Then compare several other translations of the same verses to see some of the different ways *koinonia* is translated.

Prayer

Read 1 Timothy 1:12–17 and say a prayer of thanksgiving for the salvation in Christ available to even the worst sinners, expressing gratitude that all may share eternal life.

Meditating on God's Word

Read the three letters of John, noting what is said about fellowship (and disfellowship).

FOOL

The fool says in his heart, "There is no God."

Psalm 14:1 (NIV, RSV)

When the psalmist uses the word "fool" he is not just insulting the fool's intelligence, but also commenting on his moral status. The fool is a fool because he fails to take into consideration the fact that the Almighty God exists and that God has the power, love, and wisdom to create the universe and all that is in it. Because fools do not recognize the reality of God, they do not act appropriately. There is sufficient evidence for us to know and honor God as God (Rom. 1:19–20). Those who think they know better are fools (Rom. 1:21–23). In Romans 1:24–32, Paul lists some of the evil actions of fools including gossip, disrespect, arrogance, and sexual sin.

The book of Proverbs has much to say about wisdom and foolishness. Fools are described as being arrogant and angry, lacking common sense, and bringing trouble to those around them.

> 1:7 "The fear of the LORD is the beginning of knowledge; fools despise wisdom and instruction."
> 10:1 "A foolish son is a sorrow to his mother."
> 12:15 "The way of a fool is right in his own eyes, but a wise man listens to advice."
> 14:16b–17a "A fool throws off restraint and is careless. A man of quick temper acts foolishly."
> 17:21b "The father of a fool has no joy."
> 18:2 "A fool takes no pleasure in understanding, but only in expressing his opinion."
> 18:6a "A fool's lips bring strife."
> 29:11 "A fool gives full vent to his anger." (RSV)

Matthew condemns those who call others by insulting names, such as "You fool!"

> Ye have heard that it was said of them of old time, Thou shalt not kill; and whosoever shall kill shall be in danger of the judgment: But I say unto you, That whosoever is angry with his brother without a cause shall be in danger of the judgment: and whosoever shall say to his brother, Raca, shall be in danger of the council: but whosoever shall say, Thou fool, shall be in danger of hell fire. (Matt. 5:21–22 KJV)

Raca is an insulting Aramaic word meaning "worthless" (see 2 Sam. 6:20, "vulgar") To call someone a fool and *Raca* would be to say, "You are nothing but a worthless heathen! So go to h—!"

It is not just the words used that are so hurtful, but also the anger that lurks behind them. We have little control over our feelings of anger, but we can control our speech. "Do any of you think you are religious? If you do not control your tongue, your religion is worthless and you deceive yourself" (James 1:26 GNT). We can also control our actions and attitudes. As Paul wrote to the Ephesians, it is all right to be angry, but it is not all right to sin because of that anger (Eph. 4:26–27). One can be angry occasionally without becoming an angry person. Jesus was angry when he drove the money changers out of the temple (John 2:13–17). Many positive changes in our society have been made because someone used their anger over an injustice as motivation to do something good.

On the other hand, anger unchecked is, in a sense, the equivalent of murder (Matt. 5:21–22a). Yet this sort of anger is often on display in our hearing and on social media posts. Angry eruptions and vicious name-calling are not appropriate behaviors for those who want to honor God as God. More respect is due to ourselves and to others, all of whom are created by God in his image. Let us not act like fools who do not know God, but instead ask God for his wisdom, which is "peaceable, gentle, open to reason, full of mercy and good fruits" (James 3:17 RSV).

Questions and Reflection

What do the following Scriptures say about the sources of anger?

Proverbs 15:1   Job 36:13

Ephesians 6:4   Galatians 5:19–20

The results of an angry reaction?

James 1:20   Proverbs 29:22
Proverbs 15:18   Proverbs 20:2

How to avoid anger?

Psalm 37:7–9   1 Corinthians 13:4–5
Ecclesiastes 7:8–9   Ephesians 4:30–32

How to deal with feelings of anger?

Colossians 3:8–10   Proverbs 16:32
Proverbs 14:16–17   Proverbs 29:11

How to respond to someone who is angry?

Proverbs 21:14   Proverbs 30:32–33
Proverbs 22:24–25   Ecclesiastes 10:4

Describe a time when someone was angry and another person responded in a way that calmed the angry person and avoided a volatile situation. Describe a time when someone who felt angry used that anger constructively and brought about needed change.

What have you found helpful in dealing with your own feelings of anger?

The hymn "Angry Words! O Let Them Never" (words by Horatio Palmer) has helped many to control their speech when angry. Can you think of other songs that provide similar reminders?

Compare the descriptions of God in Exodus 34:5–7 and Psalm 86:15 to the instructions to believers in James 1:19–20.

How do the following verses describe appropriate speech?

Ephesians 5:4   Colossians 4:5–6
1 Thessalonians 2:4–5   Titus 2:7–8

Use a study Bible or concordance to find the Old Testament passage quoted in 1 Peter 3:9–11. Pray that you may live as one who will inherit this blessing.

Meditating on God's Word

Read the Old Testament book of Ecclesiastes to see what "the Preacher" says about wisdom and folly, and the temporary nature of life.

FORSAKE/
FORSAKEN

My God, my God, why have you forsaken me?

Matthew 27:46 (NIV)

While helping to lead a group of college students on a trip to Oxford, England, I was asked an unusual question. The winter weather there can remain cold and cloudy for days at a time without ever warming up. One of the boys with us, unused to the English weather and miserable with the cold, dark days, asked me plaintively, "Will it ever get warm again?"

It seemed to him that the sun had completely forsaken us. However, the faithful sun was still up in the sky, pouring out its warmth and brightness toward the earth as always. Yet those warming rays never reached us at the ground level. There was something blocking the sunshine—it was those cold, dark clouds.

When Jesus was on the cross, there was something blocking the father's love—that something was all the sins of all mankind. It seemed to Jesus that God had forsaken him. Feeling the separation from God was even more agonizing to Jesus than the torture of the crucifixion.

You may have heard sermons about the pain and agony that Jesus suffered for us as he was beaten, mocked, nailed to the cross, and left to experience a slow, agonizing death. However, every person who was ever crucified, including the men on either side of Jesus, has experienced the same physical pain and suffering of the cross. There were two things that made Jesus's death different from all other crucifixions: he took upon himself the sins of all humanity throughout all history, and he was the only one who was raised from the dead after his crucifixion. What caused that pure, holy, sinless Son of the Most High God the most pain was that he experienced firsthand the horrors of the worst kinds of sin. "God made him who had no sin to be sin for us, so that in him we might become the righteousness of God" (2 Cor. 5:21 NIV). He did it because of his great love for us!

In his agony, Jesus quoted the first line of Psalm 22. He keenly felt the lack of God's presence. Because he could not feel the closeness of the Father that he had always experienced, he cried out in agony: "Why have you forsaken me?"

Perhaps at some time in your life you felt that God had forsaken you; if so, you can be assured that Jesus knows exactly how you feel.

Even when Jesus felt forsaken, we can be sure that God was still pouring out his love toward his beloved Son. Romans 8:38–39 assures us that absolutely nothing can separate us from God's love. If nothing can keep him from loving us, his sinful, wayward children, then surely there is nothing that could possibly make God forsake his holy, sinless, righteous, and beloved Son. After all, God promised, "Never will I forsake you" (Heb. 13:5 NIV).

How wonderful and comforting it is to know that God always loves us, whether or not we feel that love. Even when we have let our own sins come between us and our Lord, we can know that he is always there for us, loving us, caring for us, forgiving us when we turn back to him. We praise him for his steadfast love!

If you read all of Psalm 22 (as Jesus must have done many times before quoting the opening line) you will see that although it contains a vivid picture of the despair of a righteous sufferer, it does not end in sorrow. The writer trusts in God and remains faithful to him, and yet he must still endure a time of suffering and despair before enjoying God's deliverance.

Perhaps you have felt that God had forsaken you; you have searched your soul, confessed and repented of whatever sins were found, and yet you still suffer while sinners around you prosper. You look in faith and hope to see God's love, and feel only abandonment. If so, know that Christ understands. And even as he cried out in pain on the cross, he knew the rest of the psalm:

> You who fear the LORD, praise him! . . .
> For he has not despised or scorned
>   the suffering of the afflicted one;
> he has not hidden his face from him
>   but has listened to his cry for help. . . .
> They will proclaim his righteousness,
>   declaring to a people yet unborn:
>   He has done it! (Ps. 22:23a, 24, 31 NIV)

Questions and Reflection

For what reasons might someone feel God has forsaken them?

Look up the following passages, and give reason for God's apparent absence in each case:

Job 16:9–17	Deuteronomy 31:17–18
Psalm 6:1–3	2 Chronicles 12:5–6
Psalm 10:12–13	Lamentations 5:15–20
Psalm 13:1–2	Nehemiah 9:28

What does God's presence mean in each of these passages?

Exodus 25:22	Jeremiah 30:11
Exodus 33:5, 14	Zephaniah 3:17
Deuteronomy 31:7–8	Romans 8:31–34

Look at these passages where God promises to be (or not to be) with someone and consider the context to answer the following questions:

To whom is the promise made?

What is the reason for God's presence/absence on this occasion?

Is God's presence conditional, or are there any limitations on the promise?

Genesis 26:2–6	Joshua 7:11–13
Genesis 46:3–5	Jeremiah 42:10–16
Numbers 14:42–43	Haggai 1:12–13
Joshua 1:8–9	Acts 18:9–10

Consider a time you felt abandoned and alone, and describe what brought you comfort during that time. If you no longer feel forsaken, what has changed? Looking back, would you say that you were really as alone as you felt at the time?

Tell about a time you comforted someone who felt isolated.

Do you have a favorite hymn that reminds you of God's presence and love?

Prayer

Read 2 Corinthians 1:3–11 and think of
someone you know who is suffering. Read
the passage again and make a list of specific
things you can pray for that person. Pray.

Meditating on God's Word

The prophet Habakkuk probably wrote just before Judah was invaded by the Chaldeans (also called Babylonians), perhaps when Jehoiakim was king (2 Chron. 36:5–8 and 2 Kings 23:36–24:7). For many at that time, events challenged their understanding of God. Read the book of Habakkuk to see how he responded when it seemed God was absent and when God's response to his prayer was not what was expected.

HOPE

May the God of hope fill you with all joy and peace in believing, so that by the power of the Holy Spirit you may abound in hope.

Romans 15:13 (RSV)

A friend spent several years working in Greece. He could read New Testament Greek (*Koine*), but at first needed to spend time learning to speak Modern Greek. He tells of a time he was with a Greek friend and they were waiting to see if another friend would join them or not. The American said, "I hope he will come, but I don't think he will." And the Greek friend corrected him, "You can't say that. If you hope he will come, then you expect him and we must wait for him because he will come. But if you don't think he will come, then you must use a different word—not 'hope.'"

In Modern Greek, the word "hope" still carries the same idea of confident expectation that it does in the New Testament. In English we may use the word "hope" to express a desire without any expectation of fulfillment, but it is never used that way in Greek. When we see the word "hope" in Scripture, it refers to something in the future that is anticipated with the same certainty as if it had already happened. Looking at the context of some of the verses that use the word "hope" make it clear that the meaning is confident expectation. "Through him [Christ] you have confidence in God, who raised him from the dead and gave him glory, so that your faith and hope are in God" (1 Pet. 1:21 RSV).

We have this certainty because of who God is and what he has done:

Because God wanted to make the unchanging nature of his purpose very clear to the heirs of what was promised, he confirmed it with an oath. God did this so that, by two unchangeable things in which it is impossible for God to lie, we (Heb. 6:17–18a NIV) who have fled for refuge might have strong encouragement to seize the hope set before us. We have this as a sure and steadfast anchor of the soul, a hope that enters into the inner shrine behind the curtain, where Jesus has gone as a forerunner on our behalf. (Heb. 6:18b–20a RSV)

Our hope is that just as Christ was raised from the dead, he has given Christians new life and will one day come back to take his followers to heaven (1 Pet. 1:3–5; 1 Cor. 15:19–23). God in his love has already given us "eternal comfort and good hope" (2 Thess. 2:16 RSV) and yet that hope will not be fully realized until Christ's return: "set your hope fully upon the grace that is coming to you at the revelation of Jesus Christ" (1 Pet. 1:13 RSV). A Christian's life in Christ is both "now" and "not yet."

The word "hope" has meaning in these verses if it is understood as "confident expectation." If the idea of a "wish not likely to be fulfilled" is used, the passages would no longer make sense, and would not accomplish in the hearer what they are clearly meant to accomplish. A careful look at the context of New Testament passages using the word "hope" makes clear that its meaning includes the idea of certainty, which may not be present in the word as it is often used in other contexts today. A closer look at the Greek confirms and illustrates this different meaning that is present in Scripture. Biblical "hope" is looking forward to something with not just the possibility of fulfillment, but rather the certainty of fulfillment. Biblical hope is not wondering and wishing, but knowing and waiting.

Christians not only understand the certainty of hope (Eph. 1:18), they are expected to be willing to explain it, giving others the opportunity to share that hope: "Always be prepared to give an answer to everyone who asks you to give the reason for the hope that you have. But do this with gentleness and respect" (1 Pet. 3:15 NIV).

Questions and Reflection

What things do you wish for but do not really expect to happen? What are some of the words and phrases you use to talk about these things?

What things do you look forward to that you are confident will happen even though they have not happened yet? What sort of language do you use when talking about them?

What difference does it make in the following passages if "hope" means "wish" or if it means "expectation"?

Romans 15:4	1 Thessalonians 5:8
1 Thessalonians 4:13	1 Timothy 4:9–10

What is it that Christians hope for in these passages, and why can they be confident of them?

1 Thessalonians 4:13–14	Titus 1:2
Philippians 1:20	Hebrews 10:23
1 Timothy 6:17	1 John 3:2–3

What blessings in Christ do you have now? What blessings do you expect in the future?

The word "hope" is used frequently in the Psalms. Use a concordance to look up two or three of these passages and discuss what hope means in those verses.

In a sermon on Hebrews sometime between AD 386 and 397, an elder of the church in Antioch who was nicknamed

"Golden Mouth" ("Chrysostom" in Greek) for his eloquence said the following about hope as an anchor:

> And see how very suitable an image he has discovered: For he said not, Foundation; which was not suitable; but, "Anchor." For that which is on the tossing sea, and seems not to be very firmly fixed, stands on the water as upon land, and is shaken and yet is not shaken. . . . For the surge and the great storm toss the boat; but hope suffers it not to be carried hither and thither, although winds innumerable agitate it: so that, unless we had this [hope] we should long ago have been sunk. Nor is it only in things spiritual, but also in the affairs of this life, that one may find the power of hope great. Whatever it may be, in merchandise, in husbandry, in a military expedition, unless one sets this before him, he would not even touch the work. But he said not simply "Anchor," but "sure and steadfast" [i.e.] not shaken.[1]

Using an experience from your own life, describe how the anchor of hope could be helpful.

---

[1] John Chrysostom, "Homilies in Hebrews" 11.3 on Heb. 6:19, in *The Early Church Fathers—Nicene and Post-Nicene Fathers*, 2nd ser., vol. 14, ed. Philip Schaff (Peabody, MA: Hendrickson Publishers, 1984), 419.

Prayer

Use the ideas in Titus 2:11–14 to say a prayer
of thanksgiving to God. Then say another
prayer, this time asking for continued help
that you may learn to live as God intends.

Meditating on God's Word

Read the first letter of Peter, paying special attention not only
to the theme of hope, but also to what might be the circumstances of the ones to whom Peter wrote these words of hope.

HOSANNA

Hosanna to the Son of David! Blessed is he who comes in the name of the Lord! Hosanna in the highest!

Matthew 21:9 (RSV)

Hosanna is one of those words that cannot be adequately translated into English, so the Hebrew word is often simply written in English letters. This is called transliteration. It means that when you say "hosanna" you are actually pronouncing the original Hebrew word. In the Greek New Testament, this Hebrew word appears transliterated into Greek letters rather than being translated into a Greek word. It is one of several Hebrew or Aramaic words which appear transliterated in the Greek New Testament, including "hallelujah" (Rev. 19:1), "maranatha" (1 Cor. 16:22 GNT, KJV, NASB), and "Abba" (Mark 14:36). Since these words are not translated into Greek, most translators of the Greek Bible transliterate these words into other languages also. This means that the Hebrew word "hosanna" appears in Bibles in many different languages.

Hosanna is a shout of praise. (It is similar to hallelujah, which is sometimes translated "praise God" but the two words do not mean exactly the same thing.) Hosanna is literally, "Lord, save us," as it is translated in Psalm 118:25 (and elsewhere). It was used as a prayer (a request for salvation), but also came to be used as an acclamation (a joyous declaration of salvation). Both the prayer and the praise are present when the crowds shout "hosanna" to Jesus in Matthew 21:9, 15, and the parallel passages in Mark 11:9–10 and John 12:13.

Questions and Reflection

If you speak another language, look up verses with "halle-lujah" or "hosanna" in a Bible in that language to see if the words are translated or transliterated.

Do you know any songs that include the word "hosanna"?

Use a concordance to locate the phrase "save us" in the Old Testament prophets. Choose one passage and study it to see what is meant by salvation in that context.

Hosanna is both a request for salvation to come and a statement of salvation already here. In what sense does a Christian already have salvation? In what sense does a Christian still wait for salvation? Read the following

Scriptures, paying close attention to whether salvation is past or future in each:

Romans 10:10   Titus 3:5
1 Corinthians 1:18   Hebrews 9:28

The book of Acts tells of the first preaching of the gospel and how people responded. Use a concordance to look up the word "saved" in the book of Acts, and see how it is used.

If you were to cry "Hosanna!" today, would it be thanksgiving for salvation God has given you, or would you be seeking salvation?

Prayer

Using 2 Thessalonians 2:13–17 as a guide, pray for Christians you know but do not see often.

Meditating on God's Word

The gospels tell us of Jesus and his saving work. The book of Acts is the story of how the gospel message of salvation spread among the first converts to Christianity. Read through Acts ("skim and dip") paying special attention to themes of faith, repentance, and baptism.

JOY

For the joy that was set before him he endured the cross.

Hebrews 12:2 (NIV)

A missionary returning to the United States after many years of service to the Lord in the heart of Africa was asked, "Was it fun living in Africa?" Before answering, she thought for a moment—about the inconvenience of her outdoor kitchen and cooking over an open fire, about the bugs in the thatched roof and the dirt floor. She also thought about the many wonderful, loving people she had taught to know Christ during her years among people she had grown to love. Her heart-felt response was, "No, it wasn't fun, but there was a lot of joy in serving the people there."

Although there are times when fun and joy can be synonyms, there is a big difference between them. Sometimes one word can mean different things. A speaker intends one idea, but the hearer may understand a different meaning. It takes careful listening to communicate. The differences between "joy" and "fun" are most obvious in situations in the New Testament in which we do not expect to find joy, but there it is. We usually think of "fun" as being associated with good times that we can enjoy now and continue to laugh about as we remember the occasion of that fun. But "joy" has a much deeper side to it. One can feel joy in the direst of circumstances. Not jolly, laughter-all-the-time frivolity, but the deep-down feeling of lasting satisfaction that one gets when doing the right thing. One may be able to pretend to have fun—it tends to be superficial, but joy is not so easily faked.

The verse at the top of this page refers to Jesus, the Christ, when he was facing death. It was certainly no "fun" for him as he lay there, feeling the nails being driven into his flesh. Yet he went willingly, with joy in his heart—even knowing that he, who had never sinned, must take the sins of the whole world upon himself. It was necessary for him to accomplish this for our sake. He anticipated that there would be joy ahead that could only be experienced after he suffered. Without his death on the cross, we would have no hope of salvation. Without his resurrection from the dead, there would be no hope of our own resurrection to live with God forever. He could endure the cross with joy only because of his great love for everyone in the whole world (John 15:12–14).

Christianity is a joyful religion. Joy is at the very heart of it. God invented joy (Isa. 51:3) and he intends to give it to his people (Isa. 35:10). Jesus came to turn sorrow into joy (John 16:20–22; Isa. 61:1–3). "Gospel" means good news, not bad news! There are frequent mentions of joy connected with receiving the gospel: Jesus's parable of a man finding treasure buried in a field (Matt. 13:44); the Ethiopian eunuch (Acts 8:38–39), and the Philippian jailor with his household (Acts 16:33–34) all rejoicing at their baptisms; the joy of the churches in Phoenicia and Samaria at hearing about the conversion of Gentiles in response to the preaching of Paul and Barnabas (Acts 15:3); and Peter's reference to the joy of all who believe in Christ without having seen him (1 Pet. 1:8).

Not only does receiving God's word bring joy, but so does continuing to live by it (1 Thess. 1:6–7). Jesus wanted all his disciples (including us) to have the joy of loving and being loved by God in heaven. This kind of joy is found in our relationship with God—a relationship that is maintained by our obedience to him (John 15:10–12). The joy of the one obeying the gospel is matched by the joy of the teacher (1 John 1:3–4); it is a wonderful thing for a teacher to see students continuing to obey God (3 John 3–4).

Many places where we find joy in the New Testament, it is expected: in company with the Holy Spirit (Acts 13:52); when right things are done, not the wrong (1 Cor. 13:6) and with righteousness and peace (Rom. 14:17). However, it is somewhat surprising how frequently joy is found with suffering. Peter and John rejoiced that they were considered worthy to suffer for Christ (Acts 5:41), just as Jesus had said they should (Luke 6:22–23). There is joy in suffering because it develops Christian character (Rom. 5:3–5 RSV; James 1:2–4). And just as Jesus endured the cross for the joy to come, so Christians know that their suffering is temporary and the coming joy eternal (1 Pet. 1:6–7). All joy experienced here on earth is but a small taste of the joy to come (Rev. 19:6–7).

Sometimes a Christian's joy is clearly seen in laughter and songs of praise—such outward signs of an inner joy can be contagious. But at other times, a Christian's joy is less obvious: a subdued attitude is a more appropriate response to suffering and sorrow, but the underlying joy is still there, giving courage and strength to endure. Although joy may look different in different settings, joy does not depend on one's circumstance so much as on doing the right things and having the right attitude (1 Pet. 4:13–16). We have little control over our feelings: anger, happiness, sadness, or pride spring up inside us in response to various situations. However, attitudes are chosen: optimism, forgiveness, kindness, and gratitude demonstrate who we are, not what is happening around us.

If Christ could find joy in the cross, then surely we can be joyful in all of our own trials and tribulations. Joy comes from accepting the gospel of Christ, living in obedience to God and walking with the Holy Spirit. This is why a Christian may say, as Jesus did, "Not what I will, but what you will" (Mark 14:36 NIV).

Questions and Reflection

What distinctions do you make between the words "joy" and "fun" in your thinking and in your speech? Do you see the meaning of "happiness" as more like fun or more like joy?

Describe a time in your own life when you experienced joy and contentment while in a difficult or painful situation.

What are some songs you sing to express Christian joy?

Have you ever felt pressure to act "joyful" during difficult times when you did not feel joy? What effect did that pressure have on your attitude—was it helpful or hurtful?

Use a concordance or online Bible search tool to see how the words "joy" and "rejoice" are used in the book of Deuteronomy. What do you learn from these verses?

List the sources of joy in each of the following passages:

Matthew 13:20   Romans 15:13
Acts 14:16–17   2 Corinthians 7:6–7
Romans 14:17   Philippians 2:2

What brings you personally the greatest joy? What steals your joy?

Read Nehemiah 8:1–12. What might the phrase "the joy of the Lord is your strength" in verse 10 mean?

Prayer

Jeremiah is sometimes called the "weeping prophet" because his warnings about the sad fate that awaited God's people if they did not repent were ignored (except when he was persecuted for his preaching). Read what he says about his situation and where he found joy in Jeremiah 15:15–20. Use what he says to pray for preachers you know.

Meditating on God's Word

Read the letter to the Philippians. "Joy" is one of its better-known themes. Pay special attention to the idea of joy in times of conflict and suffering.

LORD

You shall not take the name of the LORD your God in vain: for the LORD will not hold him guiltless who takes his name in vain.

Deuteronomy 5:11 (RSV)

You may have noticed the use of capitals in the word "LORD" in the Old Testament and wondered about it. There are three capital consonants (L, R, D) and one vowel (O). The first consonant is slightly larger than the rest of the letters. When it is written that way, it stands for the personal name of God and gives importance to it.

When God gave the Israelites the Ten Commandments, he included one that told them not to use his name in vain: "You shall not misuse the name of the LORD your God" (Exod. 20:7a NIV). The name of God should not be used casually or as a meaningless expression of surprise. His name, or words derived from his name, should never be used as curse words.

Eventually, the Jews were so afraid of breaking this command that they would not even say the personal name of God.

Instead of saying his name, they substituted another name for God, *adonai* (which is the general word for "lord," whether human or divine).

Before the Greek language developed vowels, ancient languages were written with only consonants. Hebrew was written this way for hundreds of years—with just consonants and no vowels. The name for God has four letters YHWH (yod, he, waw, he) and so is sometimes called the "tetragrammaton" (which means "four letters"). Calling it the tetragrammaton is another way to avoid saying the sacred name. Even before the time of Jesus, most Jews spoke Aramaic (not Hebrew) as their first language, but learning Hebrew continued to be important so that one could read the Scriptures. All reading (even in private) was done aloud. It was more difficult to learn and to read a language written without vowels, so in the Middle Ages, a group of scholars (the Masoretes) developed vowel signs (called "points") to make the Hebrew easier to read. These vowel points were mostly added below the consonants so there was no need to recopy the sacred texts to add the vowels.

However, they had a problem when it came to adding vowels to YHWH. Making it easy to read the tetragrammaton might mean that an inexperienced synagogue reader might accidentally pronounce the sacred name. No one was supposed to say the name of God. Since the reader was to use *adonai* (a word for "lord") instead, they solved this problem by adding the vowels that go with *adonai* to the consonants YHWH. These vowels and consonants did not really go together and would be difficult to pronounce, so when the reader came to the letters YHWH, the vowel points would remind him not to say that word, but to substitute *adonai* instead. This way all would be sure not to take the LORD's name in vain.

In the Old Testament, some translators use the word "Jehovah" for the tetragrammaton; it combines in English the Hebrew consonants YHWH and the vowel pointing for *adonai*. Other translators choose to use the English word "Lord," but write it with different type to indicate that the Hebrew word being translated is the tetragrammaton, not *adonai*. In the New Testament, the Greek word for "lord" (*kurios*) may be a more general word (similar to the Hebrew *adonai*) or may specifically refer to God in the same way *adonai* is used for YHWH. It is usually translated as "lord" and can refer either to the Lord Jesus (1 Cor. 6:14; Gal. 1:19; 1 Thess. 4:16–17) or to the Lord God (James 3:9; 2 Pet. 2:9). The Christian confession of faith is that "Jesus is Lord (*kurios*)" (Rom. 10:9; 1 Cor. 12:3).

The Jews went to great lengths to show reverence for God's holy name, substituting *adonai* instead. Eventually, because the name *adonai* referred to God it also came to be considered too holy to pronounce outside the synagogue, so a devout Jew reading at home would say *ha-shim* (which means "the name") instead of pronouncing either the holy name itself or its substitute *adonai*. Perhaps this was a bit extreme, but it seems that our society today goes to the opposite extreme to be sure to show irreverence to God's holy name. As Christians, we should be careful not to use the Lord's name in a wrong way, and also see to it that both our speech and our actions are examples to others of reverence for the LORD.

Questions and Reflection

What are some names or titles children use for adults? Which of these show the most respect? Which show affection?

List some of the names for God that you have read in Scripture or heard used. Which of these show more respect, and which show affection?

In Exodus 3:1–17, God told Moses his personal name, "I am," which can mean "I exist," "I will be what I will be," or "I am what I am." This name contains the ideas of existence, presence, and activity. What does God say about himself in other places where he says "I am . . ."?

Leviticus 11:44–45   Isaiah 43:11–13
Numbers 15:40–41   Ezekiel 12:15–16
Deuteronomy 5:6–11   Zechariah 10:6

What does Jesus say about himself where he says, "I am . . ." in John?

4:25–26   10:14–15
8:58   14:6–7

Read what God says about preserving the holiness of his name in Ezekiel 36:22–27. Notice how two or three different translations handle the phrase "*adonai YHWH*" in verse 22.

The casual misuse of God's name has created several "euphemistic" forms (like "gosh" and "golly") and even the texting abbreviation "OMG." These are so familiar that we may not even think of God when we hear them. But there are other even more serious ways to misuse God's name, such as attributing things to God which are outside of his will or assigning purposes to him that are not consistent with his nature. A few examples are given below; can you think of similar ones?

Saying it was God's will that a child was killed by a drunk driver

Using business success as a sign of God's approval of sinful behavior

Prayer

Read Jeremiah 23:16–18 and pray for wisdom
to discern what is truth that comes from God
and what is falsely attributed to him.

Meditating on God's Word

Read Matthew 5–7 and consider what Jesus says about honoring God in attitudes, speech, and conduct.

MANIFOLD

Through the church the manifold wisdom of God
might now be made known.

Ephesians 3:10 (RSV)

An engine mechanic could tell you what a "manifold" is, but clearly the word is used differently in this passage. This is a verse where looking at several different translations may give a better sense of what the original meant. The New Revised Standard Version reads: "the wisdom of God in its rich variety." The Good News Translation says, "[God's] wisdom in all its different forms." Like a manifold, God's wisdom has many different aspects that work together in balance.

Think of the wisdom that was necessary to create the universe and keep it functioning. Because God's wisdom is unlimited, the universe is full of its manifold manifestations. Think of the beauty he created in spring flowers, summer landscapes, fall leaves, and winter snows and the wisdom that is necessary to hold together various ecosystems. Think of the human body and the wisdom it took to create it just so. Think of the beauty of a rosebud. Could you even imagine such beauty if God, in his wisdom, had not made it for us to enjoy?

God's wisdom providentially works in human lives to promote spiritual growth through suffering (Eph. 3:13) as well as in times of joy (Eph. 3:16–19). As the old hymn says, "God moves in a mysterious way, his wonders to perform" (words by William Cowper, 1774).

His wisdom is shown in the plans that he made for our salvation from the beginning (Eph. 3:5, 8–9). He sent his son to die for us and planned for us to be a part of his holy family (Eph. 1:5–8; 3:11–12) and assemble together regularly as his church (Eph. 1:22–23; 2:16; 4:3–6, 16; 5:24–27). It is especially through the church that his wisdom is shown (Eph. 2:19–22; 3:10; 5:32).

There are many more ways in which God's manifold wisdom is shown, and what joy his wisdom brings to his disciples (Eph. 3:20–21)! As we look around us and see what he has done for us, we feel an urgent need to fall on our knees to praise and thank him for all he has done (Eph. 1:12, 15–16), and we express our appreciation to him (Eph. 5:20) for his unending love (Eph. 2:4–5) and wisdom (Eph. 1:9–10). Most of all, we are grateful that Christ loved us enough to die in our stead (Eph. 5:2) and to establish his church (Eph. 5:29–30).

Reading several different translations may help us understand what "manifold" means in Ephesians 3:10. There are so many wonderful aspects to God's wisdom that we can explore it forever and still find more cause to marvel!

Questions and Reflection

Make list of things you see that took wisdom to create.

What songs do you know that praise God's wisdom?

Use a concordance to locate the verse that says all things "hold together" in Christ.

Can you think of other car parts that illustrate something about God's nature?

the church?
Christian living?

What image is used to describe the church in each of the following passages?

1 Corinthians 12:27	1 Timothy 3:15
Ephesians 5:31–32	Revelation 1:20
Colossians 1:24	Ephesians 2:19–22

Describe one way in which you see the church as showing God's wisdom.

What is the church doing in the following passages?

Acts 9:31	Romans 16:3–4
Acts 11:26	1 Corinthians 14:12
Acts 12:5	1 Corinthians 16:19
Acts 15:3–4	Matthew 18:15–17

Prayer

Read Ephesians 3:7–13 and from it make a
list of amazing things God has done. Say
a prayer of praise for each of them.

Meditating on God's Word

Read God's response to Job in Job 38–39 and Psalm 104, about
creation; compare what each says about God's wisdom.

MANSION

In my Father's house are many mansions.

John 14:2 (NKJV)

When we hear the word "mansion," we usually visualize a very large and fancy house that is expensively but tastefully furnished. The material wealth impresses us and our attention is drawn to the mansion. We admire the beauty of the grand dwelling. Our human minds have trouble seeing past the material blessings of this earth to see the spiritual blessings Christians will have in heaven. Of course, anything in heaven will be far superior to anything on earth. That is because those there will be with the Lord and Savior for eternity. What a blessing that will be!

Yes, God has promised his disciples a place in heaven. And we know that he always keeps his promises. There is no need to demand what he has promised. Sometimes we tell God that we are satisfied here on earth with little wealth, but in heaven we want a magnificent place. It sounds as if we think we deserve something from God! It is better to pray and sing praises to him for the many blessings he already gives us so generously every day. We can also thank him for what he has told us about heaven and what we expect there. But we do not need to tell him exactly what we want heaven to be like.

When Jesus promised his disciples a "mansion" (*monē*) in heaven, he used a word that did not carry with it the meaning of elegance or extravagance that first comes to our minds. Rather, it simply has the meaning of somewhere to live—a place to belong. The word itself does not indicate wealth, beauty, or anything large or fancy. Indeed, "mansion" in older English meant a dwelling place, a separate lodging. It is related to the word "manse," used especially in Scotland for the house of a minister or pastor—usually a simple place where everyone would be welcome. Later "manse" was used for the manor house of large estates, and so came to mean a grand house. The older, more humble meaning of "mansion" is closer to the meaning of Jesus's words in John 14:2.

"Many mansions" means there is plenty of room there for everyone to live. It is the same word used in John 14:23 when Jesus says that if anyone "loves me, he will keep my word, and my Father will love him, and we will come to him and make our home (*monē*) with him" (RSV). Jesus promised to prepare a home for those who follow him.

The word *monē*, sometimes translated "mansion," means a dwelling place—somewhere to stay and live and belong. A place to *be*. Its use in John 14 emphasizes God's presence on earth and the hope and promise of an eternal dwelling with him. And that, of course, is a grand idea.

Questions and Reflection

What do you think heaven will be like? What are your favorite songs about heaven?

There are many images and symbols in Revelation, some of which are interpreted in the book itself—some quite clearly. Look up the following verses and identify the image in each and what it represents in that context:

1:12 and 1:20	5:8
1:8 and 22:13	19:8

Other symbols are not quite so clearly explained. What might the following images represent?

Temple: 21:22	Harps: 5:8; 14:2–3
Sea of glass: 4:6; 15:2; 21:1–3	White robes: 3:4–5; 6:11

Who will be in heaven?

Matthew 7:21	Romans 8:1	Revelation 7:14
Matthew 8:11	2 Corinthians 5:17	Revelation 7:9

Search for the term "new earth" in the Bible to see what is said about the world to come.

There are many different concepts of what life after death might be like: immortality of the soul, bodily resurrection, reincarnation, and variations on each of these. Which concepts seem to be reflected in the following passages?

John 11:23–25   1 Thessalonians 4:13–17
Matthew 22:23–33   1 Corinthians 15:12–20

Christianity is sometimes criticized for placing too much emphasis on the hereafter and neglecting the present, thereby discouraging people from working to improve current conditions. How do you maintain a balance between accepting difficulties as part of this life and accepting the challenge of working to improve life for yourself and others? Do you personally find more pleasure in the blessings of God's presence in this life or in your hope for eternal life?

What reasons are given in 1 Thessalonians 4:1, 18 for describing the end times? What reasons are given in 1 Peter 4:7–8 and 2 Peter 3:11?

Prayer

Read Psalm 27:1–6. Say a prayer of thanksgiving for God's protection, safety to praise
him, and God's presence now and forever.

Meditating on God's Word

Read 1 Thessalonians, noting the significance of presence and
absence: Paul with the Thessalonians, the church with Christ, etc.

MARTYR/
WITNESS

*Grace and peace be yours from God, . . .and from
Jesus Christ, the faithful* witness

Revelation 1:4, 5 (GNT)

*I saw the woman, drunk with the blood of the saints
and the blood of the* martyrs *of Jesus.*

Revelation 17:6 (RSV)

When the early Christians faced persecution, it was inevitable that some of them would become martyrs. The meaning of "martyr" at that time was different from what it means today, even though our English word "martyr" comes from the Greek word *martys* [MAR-tous]. Do you see anything unusual about these two words? Notice that (when written with English letters) the spelling of both is almost the same. That is because this word comes almost unchanged from the Greek, through the Latin, to us. The meaning, however, has changed.

There are two meanings for the Greek word for martyr. The first meaning is "witness"—someone who testifies (as in a court of law) or bears witness to what that person knows is true. The second meaning is one who stands for something and is killed for it.

The primary meaning of the Greek word is one who speaks the truth or makes a confession of faith. The verb form is used for testifying in legal proceedings (Acts 22:5; 26:5) and a related noun (*martyria* [mart-tur-EE-uh]) means "testimony" (John 8:17: "In your law it is written that the *testimony* of two men is true" [RSV]).

Jesus's last word to his disciples (Acts 1:8) was that they were to be his witnesses; Acts tells the story of their witness. The apostles frequently used the word *martys* of themselves as Christ's witnesses (Acts 3:15, 5:32, 10:39, 13:31; 1 Pet. 5:1; 1 John 1:2; see also 1 Cor. 15:14–15.) They had been eyewitnesses to his death and resurrection, as well as having been with him, listening to his teaching and observing his conduct throughout his ministry. They testified that Jesus is the Lord, and through their witness many others became believers. All of the apostles were martyrs in the sense of "witnesses" long before any of them were killed for maintaining that testimony.

Any Christian who confesses that Jesus is Lord is a martyr in this sense. There are times when a Christian may become a martyr in the second sense: one who has suffered and even died for his or her beliefs.

The apostles lived in the Roman Empire. The emperor was considered by many to be divine, and worshiping him showed one's patriotism and loyalty to Rome. However, Christians knew that Jesus was the only Lord and the only one to be worshipped. Thus Christian witnesses who obeyed God sometimes were seen as breaking Roman law. Most of the persecutions that Christians faced in the first few centuries of the church were caused by the supporters of emperor worship. Even though persecutions were local and sporadic, enough witnesses to Christ were killed for their faith that the meaning of the word "martyr" (*martys*) changed. The word that had meant "one who bears witness" came to mean "one who died for the faith."

In Greek, the primary meaning of "martyr" is those who testify to the truth. The secondary meaning (which became the most common meaning after New Testament times) is those who are killed for their beliefs.

Like the Greek, the English word "martyr" also has two meanings. Its first meaning is, of course, the Christian one: the word describes those who were killed for their faith. It is used not only of Christian martyrs, but also for anyone who suffers or dies for any cause. But somehow the English word has lost the idea of testimony: it is now often used of anyone who suffers, even if no confession of faith or challenge to one's convictions is involved. It has developed the secondary meaning of one who exaggerates suffering to gain sympathy or praise. This second meaning of the English word is a long way from the meaning of the word as used in the Bible!

We may speak of anyone who endures suffering as a martyr, regardless of how or why they suffer. In the New Testament, the word always refers to one who is a witness and sometimes to one who is killed because of their testimony.

Questions and Reflection

Who was a witness to Jesus in each passage, and what did that person say about Jesus?

John 1:32–34   John 9:17

John 1:49   John 11:27
John 6:68–69   John 20:28

Tell about someone who has been a witness to you of who
Jesus is.

In Acts 1:8, Jesus says his apostles are to be his witnesses in
Jerusalem, all of Judea, Samaria, and to the ends of the earth.
Which apostle preached to whom in the following passages?

Acts 2:5, 14, 22   Acts 17:1–4, 16–18
Acts 8:1, 5, 14   Acts 18:1, 5–6
Acts 13:2–5, 7   Acts 28:16–17

What does Paul say in 1 Corinthians 2:1–2 about how he
preached to the Corinthians?

What does 1 Corinthians 15:2–5 say about what he said con-
cerning Christ?

Read Philippians 2:6–11 and list three things this passage
says about Jesus.

In your own words, make a brief statement about who Jesus is and what he has done. (In the early church, such statements by Christian teachers were sometimes called "the rule of faith." The wording was not fixed like the words of a creed. These statements served as a reminder of shared faith and encouraged unity.)

What recent news have you heard of modern-day Christian martyrs?

Prayer

Read John 14:8–14 and give thanks for Christ as witness to the Father and for those who have believed him and become his witnesses to us.

Meditating on God's Word

Read Acts 6:1–8:2 to see who Stephen was and what he said about Jesus. He was a witness (martyr) to Jesus and the first Christian martyr (one who died for the faith).

MIRACLE

*[Salvation] was declared at first by the Lord,
and it was attested to us by those who heard him, while
God also bore witness by signs and wonders and various
miracles and by gifts of the Holy Spirit distributed
according to his own will.*

Hebrews 2:3-4 (RSV)

We may speak of any truly wonderful event as being "a miracle," whether it is a normal event like birth or an unlikely one such as surviving a dangerous situation against all odds. The use of the word "miracle" may indicate that we know God was somehow involved in the event or that we see in it some similarity to God's miraculous actions recorded in the Bible.

When an actual definition of "miracle" is needed, it is usually explained as an extraordinary occurrence that departs from the laws of nature. However, what we understand as the laws of nature comes from an understanding of the natural order of the world that developed in the seventeenth and eighteenth centuries and is completely different from the world view common before that. People in biblical times recognized a regular order in nature, but God who created the natural world was thought not to be bound by its laws. Whether God worked within these laws or apart from them, he was at work. Some of what he did was beyond human explanation. These are the things we now call miracles.

There are three words used in the Bible for miracles: signs, wonders, and works of power. These terms occur together in Hebrews 2:3–4 (quoted above), in 2 Corinthians 12:12, and in Acts 2:22: "Jesus of Nazareth, a man attested to you by God with *mighty works* and *wonders* and *signs* which God did through him in your midst, as you yourselves know" (RSV—italics added). Each of these terms may also be used for the non-miraculous (that is, for things which can be explained by our understanding of the natural world), and each has a slightly different meaning.

The word "sign" (Hebrew *oth* [pronounced "oath"] and Greek *semeion* [see-MAY-on]) indicates the purpose of miracles: they point to or reveal something. In Genesis 17:11, circumcision is a nonmiraculous "sign of the covenant." In Deuteronomy 34:11–12 the same word refers to the extraordinary things Moses did in Egypt to show Pharaoh God's power so he would let the Israelites leave.

Signs could serve as a guarantee of God's promises (such as the rainbow in Genesis 9:13) and a reminder of his words (as in the Sabbath in Exodus 31:13). They also showed that God's messengers really brought a word from the Lord (Moses in Exodus 4:8; the apostles in Mark 16:17, 20 and Acts 5:12–14).

Jesus's miraculous signs demonstrated that he was indeed sent by God; their purpose was to create faith in him (John 6:14; 20:30–31), yet not all who witnessed Jesus's miracles believed

(John 9:16; 12:37). Jesus's signs were often the occasion for his teaching spiritual truths about himself, as when he fed five thousand on one boy's lunch before his discourse on the bread of life (John 6).

The word "wonder" (Hebrew *pele* [PEH-leh]) indicates the effect of what is done: It refers to something unusual that causes amazement. One of the names for God is "the one who works wonders" (Judg. 13:19; Ps. 77:14). The word "wonder" refers to something remarkable, and it is not always clear whether it should be considered miraculous or nonmiraculous. A nonmiraculous use of "wonder" occurs in Job 37:16, where it is used of normal weather phenomena, which are seen as under God's control. God's wonderful deeds are cause for praise (Ps. 89:5; Isa. 25:1), even though some who see his wonders still will not believe (Ps. 78:32).

In the New Testament, the Greek word for "wonders," *teras* [TEY-ras], is only used in combination with "signs," *semeion*. In the Old Testament, when the phrase "signs and wonders" is used (as in Exodus 7:3 and Deuteronomy 6:22 for what God would do/had done in Egypt) it refers to things we would call miracles, usually God's self-revelation. And yet even signs and wonders are not to be trusted if they lead people away from God rather than to him (Deut. 13:1–3). The use of "signs and wonders" in the New Testament for what the apostles did (Acts 5:12; 14:3; 2 Cor. 12:12) emphasizes their role as a part of God's revelation.

The phrase "works of power" indicates the nature of what was done: mighty deeds, usually done by God who is called the "Mighty One" (Gen. 49:24; Luke 1:49; Mark 14:62).

The Greek word for power is *dunamis,* which also can mean "strength" or "ability." (The word "dynamite" comes from *dunamis.*) In the New Testament, it usually refers to the power of God and is often translated "mighty works" or "miracles." It is used of Jesus's miracles: "What *works of power* are being done by his hands!" (Mark 6:2—translation mine; italics added here and below). Jesus also gave this power to his disciples (Luke 10:19). Christ is the "*power* of God" (1 Cor. 1:24), and Philippians 3:10 speaks of "the *power* of his resurrection." Miracles ("powers") are associated with the preaching of the Gospel (Rom. 15:19; 1 Cor. 2:4; 1 Thess. 1:5). The use of this word emphasizes that what is being done is an expression of God's power.

In Hebrews 2:4 after "signs," "wonders," and "various miracles" is added "gifts of the Holy Spirit distributed according to his will" (NIV). This phrase indicates the agency of New Testament miracles. Some gifts of the Holy Spirit are nonmiraculous (Rom. 12:6–8). Others we would call supernatural (1 Cor. 12:9–10). Even in New Testament times not everyone who received gifts of the spirit received miraculous gifts (1 Cor. 12:29–30).

Although we sometimes think of the Bible as a book of miracles, the miraculous was not a constant experience of God's people. For example, the phrase "signs and wonders" appears frequently in the Psalms, referring not to current events (when the psalm was written), but to the Exodus, which had occurred hundreds of years before. Miracles in the Bible tend to cluster around a few critical moments in salvation history. In the Old Testament, most are connected with the Exodus and the creation of the nation of Israel (the ten plagues, manna in the wilderness, the long day of Joshua, and others), but some are connected with two other periods of crisis for God's people: the threat from Canaanite religion in the days of Elijah and Elisha; and the Babylonian captivity. In between these momentous events are long periods of time when nothing miraculous is noted.

In the New Testament, there are miracles at the coming of Christ and the founding of the church. Christ himself is the ultimate miracle—born of a virgin and raised from the dead. There are several summary statements in the Gospels referring to his signs and mighty deeds and about thirty-five specific miracles attributed to him: raising the dead, nature miracles (walking on water, cursing the fig tree, etc.), casting out demons, and many healings. The apostles also performed miracles, especially healings. Jesus's miracles were considered evidence that he was indeed the Son of God (Acts 2:22). The apostles' miracles were a demonstration of the power of the resurrected Christ (Acts 3:15–16) and a confirmation of their message about him (Acts 14:3).

In between these few times when miracles occurred, there were stretches of hundreds of years in which there seem not to have been any miraculous occurrences. When this is recognized, it is not surprising that we do not see miracles today. And yet the Christian faith is founded on a miracle—God's intervention in the world on behalf of humanity. That same power of God that worked miracles in the past is available today, saving and maturing Christians (Eph. 1:19–20; 3:20). Even when there are no "miracles," God's power is at work and can accomplish more than we can pray for or understand. "The message about the cross is foolishness to those who are perishing, but to us who are being saved it is the *power* of God" (1 Cor. 1:18 NRSV—italics added).

In the Bible, miracles may be called signs, wonders, or works of power. Signs confirm that a message is from God and point people to faith. Wonders are amazing things that inspire awe. Works of power demonstrate that God is far beyond our understanding.

Questions and Reflection

What was the "sign," "wonder," or "mighty deed" in the following passages, and what was its purpose?

Exodus 3:19–20	Luke 2:10–12
Isaiah 38:6–8	Acts 15:12–18
Matthew 11:20–21	Ephesians 6:10–11

Give an example of an incident with which you are personally familiar where someone interpreted an event as a sign indicating or confirming a course of action. Do you think this was a valid interpretation of events? Why or why not?

Give an example of a time when you felt a sense of awe and wonder. Would you call what inspired that awe something miraculous? Why or why not?

Tell about some mighty work God has done in or with you or someone close to you. What was the result of God's power at work?

Read Genesis 1:1–5 and John 1:1–5.

What is the significance of "light" in each passage?

What do these passages tell us about creation?

What do these passages tell us about God?

What are your favorite hymns listing mighty and praiseworthy works of God?

Meditating on God's Word

Read John 2–6, noting the different ways Jesus's signs affected
those who witnessed them.

MODESTY

*Those parts of the body which we think less honorable we invest with the greater honor,
and our unpresentable parts are treated with greater modesty,
which our more presentable parts do not require.*

1 Corinthians 12:23–24a (RSV)

Whatever happens, conduct yourselves in a manner worthy of the gospel of Christ.

Philippians 1:27 (NIV)

The word "modesty" is rarely used in Scripture, but the concepts of humility before God, respect for others, and behaving with appropriate dignity are found throughout biblical teaching. Most discussions on modesty today center around how women dress. It is true that how a person dresses says something about who they are and what type of activities they are planning. But for both men and women modesty is far more than clothing—it refers to one's conduct and attitudes.

The concept of modesty is behind each of the Ten Commandments: the first four deal with attitude of respect and reverence toward God, the rest with how to treat other people appropriately. Much biblical teaching is about conducting oneself in ways that are fitting and bring honor to God. Speech is important, as illustrated by the many Proverbs dealing with speech (see especially 6:12–19; 10:18–21; 11:12–14; 15:1–4; 25:11; 26:17–28). Modest dress is also a part of appropriate conduct—for men as well as women: in Exodus 20:26, God says not to build an altar with steps leading up to it so "your nakedness be not exposed" (RSV); and directions for the priests' clothing include instructions for insuring modesty (Exod. 28:42–43).

The word *kosmios* (modest, suitable, respectable, dignified) is used of women's dress in 1 Timothy 2:9 where clothing is mentioned merely as an expression of one's character. The same word (*kosmios*) is also used in 1 Timothy 3:2 to describe the way a bishop should behave. James 2:1–13 discusses clothing, but not to describe how one should dress; it speaks of the importance of seeing (and treating) all persons as human beings no matter how they are dressed.

When an older woman speaks of the need for modesty in dress, younger women may hear it as a laughable criticism of style and fashion, forgetting that every era of fashion has had its modest and immodest versions. Exactly what is covered or exposed is not so significant as the character and conduct revealed by the way one dresses. Most of us realize that standards of modesty vary between cultures—especially when it comes to dress: a bikini-clad American might be shocked to see a topless African woman, but the African is shocked that an American woman would show so much leg!

Too often discussions of modesty end in acknowledging these many variations, leaving the impression that standards of modesty do not matter (because they are always subject to change) or even that modesty itself is an illusion (because there is no absolute agreement on what it is). In fact, these variations are themselves proof that modesty does matter: In every time and place, people have recognized that there is such a thing as modesty and that it does make a difference to society.

Specific rules about what is considered modest dress can be very helpful in training our children and in teaching young Christians to learn a new way to think and act. Rules, however, are limited in time and place; they must never replace eternal biblical principles. The purpose of rules is to help us learn discernment. It is easier to teach and follow a set of rules than it is to prayerfully consider what principles to apply to a given setting and then to behave in such a way that God will be honored by our speech and conduct.

It is also easier to look up a particular word in a concordance and study the passages where it occurs than it is to discern what the Bible may have to teach on a particular topic when specific words are not used. A concordance is a very handy tool (and it is good to learn how to use it), but it can never tell us everything God has to say on a subject. One must look further than the word "modesty" to see what Scripture teaches about modesty. Dress is only a part of modesty. God's people are "to walk worthily of the calling with which you were called, with all lowliness and humility, with patience, bearing with one another in love" (Eph. 4:1–2 WEB).

Standards of speech and behavior for a Christian are not determined by custom, but by our relationships with God and with one another. Appropriate dress and conduct for Christians will honor God and show humility before him. It will reflect the knowledge that all God has created is good, and it will encourage respect for one another. It will be appropriate to one's place in the church and the world, and it will project dignity consistent with one's inner nature as a child of God.

Questions and Reflection

Modesty in Conduct

In what ways is modest behavior the opposite of pride? (Is it the same as a humble attitude?)

What types of language would modesty forbid? What would characterize modest speech? Might modest speech in one setting be considered immodest in another setting?

How does a modest lifestyle relate to consumerism or to practicing sustainable living?

Modesty in Dress

What rules have you heard for length of dresses, slits and gashes, height of neckline, color of stockings, placement of bows and buttons, showing midriff skin, etc.? Which ones do you agree with (if any)?

What things have you found (do you think would be) helpful in teaching children how to dress modestly before they reach puberty?

Why do kids fight with parents over "fashion"?

How does one make the transition from enforcing rules with small children to letting older children use discernment in making their own choices? How far should a parent go in letting kids make their own mistakes?

What does clothing say about who we are and in what activities we want to engage?

Scenarios: How would you dress for a job interview? a family reunion picnic? dinner at the White House? a day at the beach? a funeral? a movie with friends?

Prayer

Read Philippians 2:1–11 and use this teaching for suggestions on what to pray for yourself and for younger Christians whom you
wish to help mature in Christ. Pray.

Meditating on God's Word

Read the beginning of Elihu's speech to Job and his compan-
ions in Job 32:1–33:18 and consider what is said here about
a person's position before God and about respect for others.

MYSTERY

The mystery hidden for ages and generations, but now made manifest to his saints. To them God chose to make known how great among the Gentiles are the riches of the glory of this mystery, which is Christ in you, the hope of glory.

Colossians 1:26–27 (RSV)

When we hear of a mystery, we usually think of a fictional story written by Arthur Conan Doyle, Agatha Christie, or some other favorite author. While reading a good murder mystery, we try to solve the mystery before it is revealed at the end of the story. To us, a mystery is something hidden, and it is difficult to learn the truth. Sometimes it is a guessing game that we may enjoy more if we cannot guess correctly.

However, when the New Testament speaks of a mystery, there is no need to guess. The "mystery" refers to something that has already been revealed, and which now should be proclaimed:

> "The mystery was made known to me . . . it has now been revealed to his holy apostles and prophets by the Spirit" (Eph. 3:3, 5 RSV)

"To make all men see what is the plan of the mystery hidden for ages" (Eph. 3:9 RSV)

"Pray also for me . . . that I will fearlessly make known the mystery of the gospel" (Eph. 6:19 NIV)

Everyone tends to read through his or her own experiences. How much better it is to allow ourselves to experience Scripture. Let each passage explain itself, and let Scripture define its own terms. These passages make it clear that the "mystery" is not something still concealed, but something revealed. The Bible is the story of God's revelation—his making himself known to his people.

Our word "mystery" comes from the Greek word *musterion* [muss-TER-ee-on]. In New Testament times there were several "mystery religions" that were quite popular. No one knows very much about them today, because the "mysteries" and their symbolic significance were revealed only to those who were initiated and sworn to secrecy. In contrast, the "mystery" of Christianity is not a secret for a select few, but was God's plan from before the beginning of time, which he has now made known to everyone by the coming of Jesus and his work (1 Tim. 3:16) for the benefit of all. The incarnation and Christ's atoning sacrifice may be difficult to understand, but they are no secret. The gospel of Jesus Christ was hidden in Old Testament times, but now has been revealed and is proclaimed in the preaching of Christ (Rom. 16:25–26). The facts of the gospel are known, and its significance is clear.

This does not mean that we fully understand God's wisdom nor how grace and faith bring about salvation; however, we do rejoice to be participants in proclaiming the revelation of

Christ, and we look forward to the time in the future when God's purposes ("mystery") will be fully accomplished (Rev. 10:7).

Questions and Reflection

There are many similarities between Ephesians and Colossians. Use a concordance to find references to "mystery" in Colossians that are similar to the verses from Ephesians (3:3, 5, 9; 6:19) quoted in this chapter.

Daniel 2:18–19 speaks of a mystery. Look earlier in the chapter to see what it is that is called a mystery and to whom it was first revealed.

Consider the following Scriptures, then describe in your own words the "mystery of the gospel" (Eph. 6:19) and why you think it would be called "a mystery."

Romans 1:16–17   2 Timothy 1:8–10
1 Corinthians 15:1–5   1 Peter 1:10–12

In 1 Timothy 3:16 there is a brief hymn about the mystery of the gospel. Take each line of this hymn and consider what it is describing, then rephrase in your own words what it means.

Can you think of more recent hymns or songs that also summarize the gospel?

It has been said that the gospel is simple enough that anyone can understand and accept God's call for salvation, and yet the Scripture is deep enough that one can study it and follow its teachings for a lifetime and still find new insights. What has been your experience with the simplicity and the complexity of biblical teaching?

Prayer

Ephesians 3 is a great chapter to study to learn more about "mystery." Verses 14–19 contain Paul's prayer for the Christians in Ephesus. Read over it, and turn it into a prayer list that you can pray for your fellow Christians. Pray.

Meditating on God's Word

Read Paul's letter to the Ephesians, paying special attention to the use and meaning of the word "mystery."

PASSION

And Jesus said to the disciples, "I have desired
[epithumein] *with a passion* [epithumia] *to eat this*
Passover with you before my passion [pathein]*."*

Luke 22:15 (translation mine)

Passion is one of the great virtues preached today. We
admire and encourage passion. If someone is passionate
about something, we think others should agree with and follow
that passion also. While we tend to think of passion as a good
thing, a quick concordance search shows that Scripture has a
more negative view of passion: Titus 3:3, "enslaved by all kinds
of passions" (NIV), and Romans 7:5, "Our sinful passions . . .
bear fruit for death" (RSV). Maybe passion is not always such
a good thing after all.

The Greek New Testament has two different words for
"passion"—*epithumia* [ep-ee-thu-MEE-uh] and *pathema*
[path-EE-mah]. (Both of them occur as either nouns or verbs,
just as the English word "desire" does.) One, *epithumia*, simply
means "desire." If the thing longed for is good, then the desire

is seen as good—such as Jesus eagerly anticipating the Passover celebration with his disciples (Luke 22:15). But if the thing longed for is bad or forbidden, then the desire is also bad—such as desire that leads to temptation and sin (James 1:14–15; see also Titus 3:3).

This word *epithumia* is used thirty-five times in the New Testament. Only half a dozen times does it have a positive or neutral sense. Human desire (passion) is usually something bad to be avoided or controlled. Paul urges Timothy to "shun youthful passions and aim at righteousness, faith, love, and peace" (2 Tim. 2:22 RSV) and warns of a time coming when "people will not endure sound teaching, but having itching ears they will accumulate for themselves teachers to suit their own passions" (2 Tim. 4:3 ESV). Strong desires often lead people in the wrong direction and may blind them to their own faults. Peter says, "Do not be conformed to the passions of your former ignorance, but as he who called you is holy, be holy yourselves in all your conduct" (1 Pet. 1:14–15 RSV). This is a topic where studying Scripture will challenge popular ideas and perhaps our own attitudes also!

Another Greek word that may be translated as "passion" is *pathema* (and the related word *pathos*). It can be translated "suffering" or "strong desire." A few times in the New Testament *pathema* means "strong desires" (Rom. 7:5; Gal. 5:24), and always refers to sinful desires. These passions are never to be indulged or pursued.

The primary meaning of *pathema* is "suffering," and it is from this usage that the death of Christ is called "the Passion." In Greek, the ideas of strong desire and suffering are linked, and the word "passion" (*pathema*) can refer to either.

In English, however, the two meanings are distinct: "passion" usually means suffering only when referring to Christ's Passion, and the meaning of "strong desire" is usually seen as very positive, regardless of what is desired.

We see suffering as something to be avoided, but in Scripture it is to be embraced as a sharing in Christ's suffering (Col. 1:24). It is a way of developing Christian character (Heb. 2:9–11). Suffering is both a preparation for Christian service and a part of ministry (2 Cor. 1:3–7).

If we wish to pursue passion as Christians, let it be according to the teaching of the apostles: may we rejoice to be counted worthy to suffer for Christ. "I count everything as loss . . . that I may know him and the power of his resurrection, and may share his sufferings [*pathema*](Phil. 3:8a, 10 RSV). As for all other desires, "Those who belong to Christ Jesus have crucified the flesh with its passions [*pathema*] and desires [*epithumia*]" (Gal. 5:24 RSV).

Questions and Reflection

What examples have you heard of the word "passion" being used of suffering?

Have you usually thought of having "a passion" for something as being a good thing or a bad thing? Has studying the verses in this article changed your ideas? If so, how?

Would you describe yourself as a "passionate person"?

If so, how has that been a good thing and how has it been a problem?

If not, are there still things about which you feel strongly or care deeply, and what are they?

Give examples (from the Bible or from modern life) where passion got someone into trouble. In each example, what besides passion contributed to the problem?

For more examples, consider these types of passion:

Sexual desire (Amnon in 2 Sam. 13)

Covetousness (King Ahab in 1 Kings 21)

Pride (Haman in Esther 3; 5–7)

Give examples where a person's desire and zeal had a positive outcome. In each example, what besides passion contributed to the accomplishment of something good?

Possible examples from Scripture might include:

Solomon building the temple (1 Kings 5; 8:18–21, 62–63)

Paul preaching the gospel to both Jews and Gentiles (Rom. 1:15; 9:2–3; 10:1; 1 Cor. 9:1–6, 12)

The Macedonian churches giving for famine relief in Judea (2 Cor. 8:1–5).

Use a concordance (with RSV, NRSV, NIV, NET, NLV, or KJV) to look up occurrences of the word "desire" in Proverbs. What do you learn about desire from these passages?

Prayer

Read what 1 Peter 1:13–21 says about choosing holiness instead of passion. Say a prayer of thanksgiving for salvation and for grace to live in holiness.

Meditating on God's Word

Read the book of Esther, noting various types of passion and also examples of restraint that play a role in the events narrated.

PERFECT

*Having been made perfect, he became the source of
eternal salvation for all who obey him.*

Hebrews 5:9 (NRSV)

A s I was teaching a class from Hebrews, a lady brought up a
problem that she had with the aforementioned verse. She
thought that if Christ had been made perfect by his suffering,
then there was a time before he suffered when he was not
perfect, therefore he must have sinned. Yet she often heard
preachers and others claim that Christ was always sinless. She
was confused because she could not reconcile the two statements. I explained that words can change their meaning over
a period of many years. In the case of the word "perfect," it has
been five hundred years since the King James Version of the
Bible was translated, using the word "perfect." We need to see
what words meant in 1611 (when they were translated) in order
to understand the verses that contain such words.

We usually think of the word "perfect" as meaning "without any flaws" and see being perfect as an unattainable goal. There are many who struggle with perfectionism—striving for what cannot possibly be achieved and yet feeling guilty for falling short. However, this is not the only meaning of the word, and it was not the primary meaning in the past. Some modern dictionaries still give the older meaning of "perfect" which is "complete" or "finished." It is this idea of completion and maturity that should be understood when the word "perfect" appears in Scripture. It is the word used to translate the Greek word *telios*, which means "complete" or "mature."

There are several other verses where we can see that "perfect" meant "complete" to the translators of the King James Bible, such as Acts 3:16, when the lame man was completely healed, and Acts 24:22, where it says Felix had a more complete knowledge of the Way. Even though "perfect" now usually means something different, there are modern translations that still use "perfect" in these verses.

Another example of a word that has changed meanings is "prevent." To us that word means to keep something from happening, as "to prevent an accident." But five hundred years ago, that word meant "to go before" ("pre" = "before" and "vent" = "to go," so "prevent" = "to go before") not "to keep from happening." Today we use the word "precede" to mean "to go before" ("pre" = "before" and "cede" = "to go," so "precede" = "to go before"). Thus "I prevented the dawning of the morning" (Ps. 119:147 KJV) meant "I got up before dawn." Five centuries ago, "prevent" meant "to go before" and "perfect" meant "complete," "mature," and "finished"; but "perfect" did not mean "flawless" or "sinless."

The last verse of 2 Corinthians 5 assures us that our Lord indeed never sinned; instead, he completed the job God sent him to earth to do. That job was to reconcile humanity to God by the blood of his atoning sacrifice.

> Therefore, if anyone is in Christ, the new creation has come: the old has gone, the new is here! All this is from God, who reconciled us to himself through Christ and gave us the ministry of reconciliation: that God was reconciling the world to himself in Christ, not counting people's sins against them. And he has committed to us the message of reconciliation. We are therefore Christ's ambassadors, as though God were making his appeal through us. We implore you on Christ's behalf: Be reconciled to God. God made him who had no sin to be sin for us, so that in him we might become the righteousness of God. (2 Cor. 5:17–21 NIV)

Christ completed all that the Father sent him to accomplish. After his death, burial, and resurrection, there was nothing more for him to do except to ascend back home to the Father. God's plan had become mature, and it is now up to people to accept what Jesus has done and tell others about this reconciliation.

When you see the word "perfect" in Scripture, think of it as including the idea of finishing what one has started and being faithful to the end. It is used to translate the Greek word *telios*, which is often used in passages urging Christians to grow in maturity (such as Eph. 4:13; Col. 1:28; Heb. 5:14). When the verb form of this same Greek word is used, it is often translated "complete" or "finished," as in Jesus's final words from the cross (John 19:30; also in 2 Tim. 4:7; Rev. 15:1). If you substitute the word "complete" or "mature" for the word "perfect" you may find it enriches your understanding of the passage.

The lady who had the problem with the two different statements was relieved and thankful that she no longer had a problem, but now understood. Christ is and always has been completely without sin; his work of reconciling us to God was completed only in his suffering.

Questions and Reflection

Have you ever felt pressure to be "perfect" because you are a Christian?

Is it reasonable to expect perfection from yourself (or anyone else)?

Do you see any potential problems with viewing someone else as being "perfect"?

Many persons struggle with perfectionism—the need to get everything just right in order to feel valuable/worthy/loved. Do you see any difference in trying hard to do something to please someone you know already loves you and trying to do something to earn someone's love?

The verb form of *telios* can be translated "perfect," "finish," or "complete." What was completed or finished in each of the following passages that use this word?

    Luke 2:39   Luke 18:31
    Matthew 7:28   2 Corinthians 12:9
    Matthew 11:1   James 2:8

In the following passages, many translations use the word "perfect" for *telios*. Try substituting the word "complete" or "mature" to see how well each different word might fit the context and how it helps to understand the meaning of the passage.

    Matthew 19:21   Colossians 3:14
    Romans 12:2   1 Corinthians 13:9–10

Consider what Ephesians 4:11–16 has to say about maturity, and answer the following questions:

How does one gain maturity?

How does one recognize maturity versus immaturity?

What are the advantages of maturity?

From Hebrews 4:14–16 list three things about Jesus, and then explain the significance of each for our relationship with him.

Explain the significance of Christ's sinlessness for our salvation. See 1 Peter 2:22–24.

Prayer

Read Ephesians 2:4–10. Say a prayer of praise to God for salvation in Christ; a prayer of thanksgiving for salvation that depends on Christ's sinlessness, not our own; a prayer that we may live in a way that reflects the gift of salvation.

Meditating on God's Word

Read Hebrews 1–5 and consider Christ—his nature, his ability to reconcile humans to God, and what his sacrifice means.

PERSECUTION

When they heard this they were enraged and wanted to kill them.

Acts 5:33 (RSV)

*Blessed are those who are persecuted for righteousness'
sake, for theirs is the kingdom of heaven.*

Matthew 5:10 (RSV)

The word "persecution" (or "persecute") is used very few
times in the New Testament. However, a concept can be
present even when a particular word is not used. There are
many places in the Bible where there is a reference to some type
of persecution even when the word is not used. For example,
Jeremiah 20:1–2, Acts 5:17–18, 40, and 1 Peter 3:13–17 all speak
of persecution without using the word.

Many think that persecution of Christians began at the
beginning of the church and was constant and widespread
from then on. That was not exactly the situation.

The early persecutions of the church were generally
directed toward individuals and not toward the whole church.
For example, the Sanhedrin (the ruling council of the Jews)
ordered Peter and John not to speak in the name of Jesus, but

they did not make any legal pronouncements against the whole church (Acts 4:18–21). The apostles determined to obey God rather than men, and were soon arrested for disobeying the council's order (Acts 5:17–32). Many members of the Sanhedrin wanted to put them to death, but Gamaliel persuaded the authorities to let them go, just in case the apostles were right (Acts 5:33–40). Not only did this save their lives, it also meant the gospel had some legal standing as a part of Judaism. Peter and John were severely beaten with whips before they were released, but they rejoiced that they were able to suffer disgrace for the name of Jesus and they continued preaching Jesus publicly (Acts 5:41–42). The whole church responded to the start of this persecution by praying for boldness (Acts 4:23–31).

Persecutions continued to be local and sporadic rather than widespread and constant. The church at Antioch was founded by believers fleeing persecution but enjoyed a long period of peace (Acts 11:19–26). The church in Iconium had trouble from the very start (Acts 14:1–7), and enemies of the gospel there followed Paul to Lystra and almost killed him (Acts 14:19–20). These early persecutions came primarily from fellow Jews, often motivated by bitter jealousy (as in Acts 5:17). Later, Roman officials were the persecutors.

Persecution in the Old Testament

Persecution of God's messengers did not begin with the church. Many of the prophets of the Old Testament were persecuted for their preaching. See Hebrews 11:35–38 for a partial list of what was done to some of them. They were tortured, mocked, and whipped. Some were tied up and put in prison. Some were even stoned or killed in other ways. Jesus spoke of this in a parable about a vineyard (Mark 12:1–12) and places his own death in this tradition of persecution.

Persecution in the New Testament

The apostle Paul himself persecuted Christians before he was converted to Christ. He "was ravaging the church, and entering house after house, he dragged off men and women and committed them to prison" (Acts 8:3 RSV). And later, "still breathing threats and murder against the disciples of the Lord, went to the high priest and asked him for letters to the synagogues at Damascus, so that if he found any belonging to the Way, men or women, he might bring them bound to Jerusalem" (Acts 9:1–2 RSV). It was on this journey that the Lord appeared to him in a vision (Acts 9:3–9). Three days later, Paul was with the very people he had come to persecute and was preaching about Jesus (Acts 9:18–22). It was not very long until he himself began to be persecuted (Acts 9:23). Second Corinthians 11:24–27 lists some of what he endured: he was whipped, beaten, stoned, left for dead, and imprisoned, among other persecutions.

Persecution by the Romans

The gospel often received a favorable reception from officials in many parts of the Roman world: the Centurion (a high-ranking military commander) Cornelius in Caesarea (Acts 10), the proconsul (provincial governor for Rome) in Cyprus (Acts 13:12), the Areopagus (high court) in Athens (Acts 17:34), and the Asiarchs (wealthy civic and religious leaders) in Ephesus (Acts 19:31). Sometimes Roman officials chose to ignore Jewish persecution of Christians as being a matter for Jews to settle among themselves, as did Gallio, proconsul of Achaia in Corinth (Acts 18:12–17). At other times, they were instruments of persecution, as when merchants in Philippi who had a grudge against Paul and Silas found a way to have them beaten and imprisoned by the Romans (Acts 16:16–24).

Later, persecution by the Romans took a different form. Rome considered her emperors to be divine; therefore, they should be worshipped. The Christians declared that Jesus was Lord. Although the potential for conflict was great, Rome was usually content to allow Christians their strange religious ideas. At times, however, an enemy could use a Christian's refusal to participate in emperor worship to confiscate the property of Christians and have them imprisoned. And occasionally officials in some part of the empire, feeling the need to convince Rome of their loyalty and devotion, would demand that everyone—even Christians—say that the emperor was Lord and burn a little incense in his honor. Anyone who did not obey would be tortured and perhaps killed. But for Christians, saying "Caesar is Lord" would be to deny that Jesus is Lord and to forfeit their inheritance in heaven—they would be considered apostates, no longer a part of the church. Although this type of persecution was more common after New Testament times, it may provide the background to the book of Revelation.

Application Today

Matthew 5:10–12 reminds us that persecution may take other forms than infliction of physical suffering. However, the occasional negative reaction to one's faith should not be confused with persecution. Even repeated inconvenience caused by those who do not appreciate one's religious views should simply be considered a natural consequence of being around people who disagree. But in some parts of the world Christians today face very real danger of persecution. This happens because of laws limiting freedom of religion, because there are persons determined to harm Christians and churches, and sometimes because those who do not understand Christianity think they are doing right by opposing it and persecuting followers of Jesus. In some parts of the world today it is very dangerous to confess, "Jesus is Lord."

We rightly want to pray for the safety of Christians everywhere. Let us also pray that those in challenging and dangerous situations will have the faith and courage to pray as the first disciples did in Acts 4:29–31, asking God to enable them to speak his word with boldness. Let us also pray for the persecutors, as Jesus taught in Matthew 5:44. May the faith of the persons in Hebrews 11 live in us, and especially in those Christians who are serving the Lord in the midst of danger.

Questions and Reflection

When Christians feel persecuted, what should be their attitude toward the situation and toward their tormentors? Here are some passages to consider:

Daniel 3:14–18	John 15:20–21
Amos 7:12–17	John 17:14–17
Philippians 1:15–18	Matthew 10:16–20
Psalm 109:3–9	1 Peter 3:14–16

Before his conversion, Paul (also called Saul) persecuted Christians, as described in Acts 9:1–2. Why might he have done this? (Consult his own account of events in Acts 22:3–5 and Acts 26:4–11 for clues.)

Read Jeremiah 26 to answer the following questions about a time Jeremiah was persecuted:

What was Jeremiah's message? (verses 1–6)

Why do you think the priests wanted to kill Jeremiah when they heard this? (verses 7–9)

What about the other prophets?

All the people?

What might have motivated Jeremiah to respond as he did in verses 12–15?

What role did "certain of the elders" (verses 17–19) have?

Why do you think they spoke as they did?

How did the trial end? (verse 24)

Have you heard of any recent incidents that might be considered persecution of Christians? If so, do they involve someone seeking to harm Christians or attack the gospel message? Is the term *persecution* appropriate to the situation or would it be an exaggeration? How serious is the threat? What might be the "ideal" response to these situations?

If the church in your area were to experience a time of persecution, what songs and hymns do you think might give you the most comfort and encouragement?

Prayer

Read Acts 4:24–31 for an example of how to pray when facing persecution. Take a few moments to pray for Christians currently being persecuted—pray both for their physical safety and their spiritual strength.

Meditating on God's Word

Read Jeremiah 35–39 for an account of Jeremiah's difficult ministry in the dangerous times leading up to the capture of Jerusalem by the Babylonians (Chaldeans). Watch for the themes of trust in God and obedience to his word.

PRAISE

Every day I will bless thee, and praise thy name
for ever and ever.

Psalm 145:2 (RSV)

Many psalms start with "I will praise the Lord" or "Let us praise the Lord" as a call to others to join in the praise. But that phrase is not usually repeated. Instead, it is followed by a list of God's praiseworthy characteristics and deeds. The psalmist may tell you he is about to give praise; then he spends much more time doing it rather than talking about it.

Did you ever notice the way a couple in love talk about each other? He will tell you how beautiful she is, how clever, and how sweet. Even if he is usually quiet, he cannot seem to stop telling you about her accomplishments and about the charming things she said to him. She will tell you how kind and thoughtful he is, and such a hard worker. They will praise each other all day long. But probably neither one will tell you they are going to praise their beloved—each is too busy talking about the other. That is what praise is. We do not praise God by saying we will praise him, but by telling how wonderful he is and what great things he has done.

Praise and thanksgiving often go together, but they are not the same thing. Praise is saying great things about someone; thanksgiving is showing appreciation for how much that person has meant to you. If someone is introducing his favorite professor to an academic audience, he might say something like, "In addition to having written several well-known books and many significant articles, he has taught generations of scholars to be thorough in their research, precise in their presentation, and rigorous in challenging their own conclusions." Now that is praise. When the one making introductions starts talking about how this professor influenced the course of his own life and inspired him to become the respected scholar he now is, then it is not so much praise that is expressed, but gratitude.

Praising God often does flow naturally into thanksgiving—and we should give thanks to God for what he has done for each of us personally. However, if we do not also praise God for who he is and what he has done quite apart from what it means to us, then we risk losing sight of his power and glory. It is only a small bit of God's strength that has touched any one of us. He is far beyond our understanding, and we should not forget to respect that.

There are some special words of praise that apply to God alone. We should remember these words often as we praise the Lord. We can praise God as the creator of the world and all the magnificence and variety in it. He is the source of life and joy (Gen. 2:7; Deut. 16:15). Because he is unlimited in creative power, creating all that comes into existence, God may be called *omnificent* (meaning "all-creative"). God is not only creator, but also king over all nature and all nations (Isa. 43:15–21), and even has power over death (Isa. 25:8). Because he is all-powerful, with unlimited authority, he is called *omnipotent*. God is not only lord over everything, but he is everywhere, at all times. He sees and knows everything that happens anywhere (Ps. 139:1–12). Because God is always present in all places, he is called *omnipresent*. God not only sees all, but he has infinite awareness, understanding, and insight. He is wise and the source of all wisdom (Job 28:12–28; James 1:5). As all-wise and all-knowing, he is called *omniscient*.

The more you think about who God is and all that he has done (Ps. 111), the more natural it is to praise him. We need to get beyond expressing our intentions to praise and actually give praise. We need to practice praise as something more than thanksgiving. To praise God is to speak the truth about his power and love. It reminds all who hear of who God is and why trusting him is reasonable and wise. It reminds us of who we are in relationship to God. And maybe God smiles to hear it.

> The LORD is gracious and merciful,
>   slow to anger and abounding in steadfast love. . . .
> The LORD is faithful in all his words,
>   and gracious in all his deeds. . . .
> He fulfills the desire of all who fear him,
>   he also hears their cry, and saves them.
> The LORD preserves all who love him;
>   but all the wicked he will destroy.
> (Ps. 145:8, 13b, 19–20 RSV)

Questions and Reflection

To better learn the difference between praise and thanks-giving, read the following passages from the Psalms, and classify each as either praise or as thanksgiving. Remember that praise is about someone else, and thanks is about your personal benefit.

Psalm 18:16–19   Psalm 95:2–5
Psalm 47:7–8   Psalm 98:1–3
Psalm 50:1–2   Psalm 107:1–3
Psalm 56:12–13   Psalm 118:21

Most people find it difficult to praise God without thanking him.

1. Why do you think that is?

2. Why might it be important to spend some time praising God without giving thanks?

Do you have a favorite passage of praise? A favorite hymn?

Count how many times the word "praise" is used in Psalm 135. (It may vary slightly by translation.) Then make a list of reasons this psalm gives for why God should be praised.

Prayer

Make a list of three things God has done
for you for which you are thankful.

First, thank God for each of them.

Next, look at each item on the list to see
how it shows something about the nature
of God, and write beside each item the
characteristic(s) of God it reflects.

Finally, give praise to God for that trait without mentioning how it has affected you.

Praising the Lord may be described as turning a spotlight on God (and off yourself). Keeping this idea in mind, write a few sentences of praise. (Make it a poem if you like!)

Meditating on God's Word

Read chapters 1–7 of the book of Daniel, noting reasons for praising God, who praised whom, and how praise was given.

PREDESTINE/ PREDESTINATION

*For those whom he [God] foreknew he also predestined
to be conformed to the image of his Son . . . and those
whom he predestined he also called.*

Romans 8:29–30 NRSV

When one hears the verb "predestine" or noun "predestination," one tends to think of his or her eternal destiny as already having been determined with no possibility of change. This idea, however, is not what the Bible teaches.

In Scripture, the word "predestine" refers especially to God's plan in regard to Christ. God decided before the ages to save human beings through the death and resurrection of Jesus. In 1 Corinthians 2:7, Paul describes his preaching about Jesus's crucifixion: "But we impart a secret and hidden wisdom of God, which God decreed [predestined] before the ages for our glorification" (RSV). What God ordained long ago is now revealed and taught.

With reference to Christians, Paul wrote that God "*destined* us for adoption as his children through Jesus Christ"

(Eph. 1:5 NRSV—italics added) and that "In Christ we have also obtained an inheritance, having been *destined* according to the purpose of him who accomplishes all things according to his counsel and will" (Eph. 1:11 NRSV—italics added). Notice that these statements are collective: "we" and "us," not "I" and "me." This is not predestination of individuals but of a people. The people are those who are "in Christ." In Ephesians 1:12 the same "we" who were predestined are the "we who first hoped in Christ" (RSV). God does not choose who will be in Christ, but he chooses those who are in Christ to be his inheritance.

This might be compared to an association that has rules for membership. The qualifications of members are set in advance, but this does not specify which individuals will be included. Long before Jesus's crucifixion, God planned (predestined) that salvation would come through his death to those who would believe in him. There are many passages that speak of God's desire that everyone be saved (John 3:16; 1 Tim. 2:3–4). However, only those in Christ receive the blessings promised for those who are in Christ (Gal. 3:26–27; Eph. 1:3, 3:6; 2 Tim. 2:10).

Two thousand years of religious history now stand between us and the Scripture. Different ideas developed during this time may influence how we understand the Bible, but it does not change the meaning intended—and it is that original meaning that we seek to understand. History may inform and enlighten our understanding, but sometimes it may obscure the meaning of Scripture.

The word *pro-orizo,* translated as "predestine," has two parts. The prefix *pro-* means before, and the root *orizo* has the basic meaning of "to set a limit" (as in Acts 17:26). (The word "horizon" comes from *orizo;* the horizon marks the boundary where the land or sea meets the sky.) *Orizo* can also mean, "to plan to do something" (as in Acts 11:29), "to choose a date" (Acts 17:31; Heb. 4:7), or "to designate/declare someone to be something" (Rom. 1:4; Acts 10:42). So the word *pro-orizo* would mean "to define beforehand" or "to mark off the boundaries in advance." The prefix *pro-* may also serve as an intensifier: "to make definite plans in advance."

The word *pro-orizo* ("predestine") occurs six times in the New Testament: Acts 4:28; Romans 8:29–30 (twice); 1 Corinthians 2:7; Ephesians 1:5, 11. Each of these passages has the idea that God planned ahead for what happened. Although these verses are used to support the idea that God has predetermined which individuals will be saved, apart from any human choice or action, there is nothing in any of these passages that requires them to be understood in this way. The debate as to how much room there is for human choice within God's plans comes more from our difficulty in understanding God's power (and his love) than from any ambiguity in Scripture. God always acts in a way consistent with his own nature and will. Humans do not always act in ways consistent with God's will.

When the first disciples spoke of the Roman and Jewish leaders as having done whatever God's hand and plan "had predestined to take place" against his "holy servant Jesus" (Acts 4:27–28 NRSV), it does not indicate that they thought every detail was predetermined by God in such a way that individuals had no choice in the matter. Rather, it means that they knew that God had planned ahead for everything that had happened, that Jesus's crucifixion and resurrection were God's plan for their salvation, and that they could safely trust in him and his plans no matter what might happen next.

Questions and Reflection

What difference (if any) does it make to how you think and live if you believe that God determined your eternal destiny long ago, apart from anything you do?

Is there any difference between saying that God saves those who choose to obey him and saying that one can earn salvation by what he does (or does not do)? Explain.

Look up 1 Corinthians 2:7 in three or four different versions to see how *pro-orizo* is translated.

Look up Ephesians 1:11–12 in the Easy to Read Version or the New Century Version and compare to the version you normally use.

Which of the following passages indicate that God has already set a course that cannot be altered, and which show God changing his mind (and why)?

Ezekiel 24:14	Jeremiah 23:20
Numbers 23:19–20	Zechariah 8:14–15
1 Kings 13:6	1 Chronicles 21:15
Isaiah 38:1–6	Jeremiah 26:13

What blessing is there for those "in Christ" in each of the following passages?

Ephesians 2:13	1 Corinthians 1:4
Ephesians 3:6	Galatians 3:28–29
Romans 3:24	2 Timothy 1:1
Romans 8:1	1 Peter 5:10

Prayer

Read Deuteronomy 30:15-20, and pray
that your family will choose life and good,
rather than turning away from God.

Meditating on God's Word

Read Jeremiah 13–15 on the purpose of prophecy/preaching, paying special attention to references to a change of direction.

REDEEM

You are worthy . . . for You were slain, and have
redeemed us to God by Your blood.

Revelation 5:9 (NKJV)

Anyone who has visited Rome has probably had a tour of the ancient forum. Pictures of it are sometimes familiar even to those who have not been there. Every city in the Roman world had a forum; Greek cities called it an *agora* (ah-gor-*AH*). It was sort of a combination mall, farmer's market, and city park with the courthouse and county clerk's office there too. Just about anything imaginable was probably bought and sold at the forum or *agora* at one time or another—even slaves. In fact, the Greek word for "to buy" is *agorazo* (ah-gor-AH-dzo). This word is used for buying goods, services, or slaves; it can also be used of buying a slave's freedom.

Sometimes in the ancient world, a friend or relative might buy a slave to set him free. More often the slave himself would earn and save enough money to buy his own freedom. The way this was usually done was for the slave to give the money to the (pagan) priests, who would then pay the owner the price of the slave. The legal documents would reflect that a god is making the purchase. This would protect the former slave from any attempts by the former master or his heirs to reassert ownership. Legally, the slave now belonged to the god; practically, he was now a free person.

In the New Testament, one of the words usually translated "redeem" is *agorazo* (or the related word *exagorazo*). Christ buys people back from the "curse of the law" (Gal. 3:13). The phrase "bought with a price" in 1 Corinthians 6:20 and 7:23 (RSV) echoes the language of legal documents freeing a slave, but there is a difference. This purchase was not made with money that had been given to the priest for that purpose, but the price was paid entirely by the priest himself, and paid with his own blood (Heb. 9:11–12).

Understanding a little of the cultural setting of the New Testament helps us to understand redemption better. When Christ redeems us, it is quite different from trading in a coupon or frequent flyer miles, and somewhat closer to the idea of buying something back from a pawnshop. However, it is a person who is redeemed, not a thing. A closer parallel might be paying the ransom of someone who has been kidnapped.

Perhaps the most familiar use of the word "redeem" outside of Scripture is in the phrase "redeem oneself"—that is, to set things right after making a mistake and to make oneself look good again. In some situations, one can redeem oneself in the eyes of others—and this is a very good thing when it is done. However, this is the opposite of what the Bible means by redemption. If people could redeem themselves, the law would not be a curse and Jesus would not have needed to die.

In the ancient world, even if a slave had earned money to buy his own freedom, he could not do it without the help of the gods. In the same way, we cannot be redeemed without Jesus—and we do not have anything to trade for our own freedom; it is Jesus who pays the full price.

Questions and Reflection

Give an example of a time when someone messed up, and then tried to redeem themselves. Was that person able to set things right on their own, or did they require help?

See "redeem" in a dictionary. Compare various definitions given to the meaning of 1 Corinthians 6:20 and 7:23. Describe in your own words what it means to be "bought with a price."

Look up the following verses to answer each question:

What are Christians redeemed/rescued/saved from?

1 Peter 1:18   Galatians 1:4   Titus 2:14

Who redeems people?

John 3:17   Acts 4:10–12   Titus 2:11; 3:5–6

How are believers redeemed?

Ephesians 1:7–8   Hebrews 9:12

There are many songs and hymns that celebrate our salvation in Christ. Do you know any that use the words "redeem" or "redemption"?

1 Thessalonians 5:9 says Christians are appointed "to receive salvation through our Lord Jesus Christ" (NIV). How do they receive this gift?

Acts 10:43   Acts 11:18   Acts 8:12
Acts 16:31   Acts 16:15   Acts 18:8
Acts 3:19   Acts 22:16   Acts 2:38

In each passage, find a characteristic of Christ that makes him able to redeem us:

John 5:17–18   Hebrews 4:15   Romans 6:9

Ephesians 4:1 says, "live a life worthy of the calling you have received" (NIV). What is the difference between earning salvation and living up to salvation already obtained?

Prayer

Read Colossians 1:9-14 and use Paul's description of his prayers for Christians dear to him to help you pray for yourself and those you love.

Meditating on God's Word

Read Exodus chapters 11–13 as background and Numbers 3:11–13, 40–51 on the "redemption of the firstborn." See also Numbers 18 on what it would mean to be a Levite, substituted for the firstborn sons of Israelites.

REPENT

None of them repent of their wickedness, saying,
"What have I done?" Each pursues their own course
like a horse charging into battle.

Jeremiah 8:6 (NIV)

Have you ever seen a child forced to apologize for something? He looks sheepish, eyes downcast, and mumbles, "I'm sorry." You wonder if any of the remorse is for what he did in the first place, or if he's only sorry he got caught and had to apologize. Do not mistake this for repentance.

Even if there is true remorse, both sorrow for the action and regret for the trouble and pain it may have caused, remorse is just a feeling. Feelings are temporary and unreliable. Remorse will sometimes, but not always, prompt repentance: "Godly sorrow brings repentance that leads to salvation and leaves no regret, but worldly sorrow brings death" (2 Cor. 7:10 NIV). Repentance is much more than remorse or regret.

The Greek word for "repent," *metanoeo*, means to change one's mind. A change of how one thinks involves both looking at things differently and reacting differently. It is a reformation of will and purpose. One may regret former ways of thinking, but the new way of acting is a far more important part of repentance. In Matthew 3:8, John the Baptizer preaches: "Produce fruit in keeping with repentance" (NIV). When a person repents, the change can be seen.

One of the Hebrew words for "repent" is *shuv*, which means to turn or return. It is sometimes used to mean a literal change of direction. For example, King Nebuchadnezzar briefly lifted his siege of Jerusalem when Pharaoh's army marched out to aid them, but in Jeremiah 37:7–8, Jeremiah warns that the Egyptian army is "about to return [*shuv*] to Egypt, to its own land" (v. 7, RSV). "Then the Babylonians will return [*shuv*] and attack this city" (v. 8, NIV). The Egyptians are turning around and going back home; the Babylonians will resume their previous attack on the city. In each case, there is a turning from one thing and going back to what had been before. Because the word *shuv* has the idea of going back to something done before, it is sometimes translated as "again" (Jer. 6:9; 18:4; 36:28); it is also used of "restoring" fortunes (Jer. 48:47; 49:6, 39; 50:19). The word *shuv* is also used metaphorically of changing loyalties, as in Jeremiah 3:19, where God says to his people, "How gladly would I treat you like my children . . . I thought you would call me 'Father' and not turn away [*shuv*] from following me" (NIV). It is frequently used in the call for people to turn away from evil and turn to God: "If you return [*shuv*] . . . to me you should return [*shuv*]" (Jer. 4:1 RSV).

The use of the word *shuv* ("turn" or "repent") is especially interesting in the book of Jeremiah. In spite of their history, there is some hope that the people may repent: "When people fall down, do they not get up? When someone turns away [*shuv*], do they not return [*shuv*]?" (Jer. 8:4 NIV). This would prevent the coming disaster of defeat and captivity; both God and the prophet lament that the people do not respond to the repeated calls for repentance (Jer. 18:11–12; 25:5–7; 26:3–5; 35:15; 36:3–7; 44:5). Ultimately, there is a point at which even true repentance will no longer avert the consequences of sin (Jer. 23:20; 30:24). The people did not repent, and they were defeated by the Babylonians and taken into captivity.

The most common uses of the word *shuv* in Jeremiah is in connection with the desire of the captives to return from Babylon (Jer. 22:27; 44:14); the impossibility of doing so—"Weep not for him who is dead, . . . weep bitterly for him who goes away, for he shall return [*shuv*] no more to see his native land" (Jer. 22:10 RSV); and the promise that some of their children would one day return. The Lord says: "I myself will gather the remnant . . . I will bring them back [*shuv*] to their fold" (Jer. 23:3 NRSV). It is God who causes the Israelites to return from Babylonian captivity (Jer. 29:14; 30:3; 32:37–38); he will restore their fortunes again (Jer. 30:18; 31:23; 32:44; 33:26).

The language of turning away from evil and toward God is very similar to the language of captives returning home. The call to repent is not just a call to turn away from something, but calling people back to God—back home where they belong: "Bring me back [*shuv*] that I may be restored [*shuv*], for you are the LORD my God" (Jer. 31:18 ESV).

John the Baptizer spoke much like the Old Testament prophets. He taught a "baptism of repentance" (Mark 1:4) in which a person turns to God, and God purifies and changes that person's nature in baptism. Later, Christian baptism is into

Christ (Acts 2:38; Rom. 6:3). Faith, repentance, and baptism remain essential to Christian conversion. Repentance is not just a turning away from sin, but returning to the God who created us and loves us.

Repentance is an essential part of the conversion process by which one becomes a part of the family of God. But since sin continues to tempt Christians, there is often a continuing need for repentance in some areas of life even after the decision has been made to obey God.

There are many aspects to repentance. It begins with a recognition of the wrong committed (Ps. 51:3–4) and admission of guilt (1 John 1:8–10). Sometimes a public retelling (confession) is appropriate: public sin should be confessed publicly; private sin, privately; secret sin, secretly. A by-product of this recognition is remorse for the action and its consequences (Ps. 51:10–11; Jer. 31:19), which usually should be expressed in an apology to those affected. Repentance is more than remorse and an apology; it must include a reformation in thinking and a turning from previous behaviors to new ways of reacting. Usually, there needs to be some form of restitution (Lev. 6:1–7; Luke 19:8). Repentance makes reconciliation with God possible (Ps. 51:12–15; 2 Cor. 5:18–19), but reconciliation with others depends not only on the one who has repented, but also on the willingness of others, so it may not be possible. (Even if some degree of reconciliation is achieved, it can take some time afterward to rebuild relationships.) True repentance will also include resolutely following the new course (Acts 26:20; Luke 3:8–9). The essence of repentance is turning to a new way of thinking and acting.

Twelve-step addiction recovery programs were first developed by Christians from Scripture and often include a much more complete understanding and practice of repentance than some church literature on conversion does. Regret is but a small part of repentance. In repenting, one turns in a different direction. It is as if one were in a sailboat going in one direction, and then turned 180 degrees to go the other way. Once the new direction is set, minor adjustments may frequently need to be made to stay on course. One does not turn all the way around to go in the old direction again, but continues to head in the new direction. To change one's heart and mind involves determination to do things differently. Repentance includes a change in behavior.

Questions and Reflection

List some of the things you have heard people say by way of apology. Which ones sounded like they might be sincere, and which seemed to be lacking something?

Give examples of someone making amends, or restitution, following repentance.

Luke 3:8–14 describes what is involved in repentance. List each group of people addressed and what repentance would look like for each of them.

Read the following passages to see what followed repentance in each case.

Matthew 21:29	Acts 2:38	Hebrews 6:1
Luke 17:3–4	Acts 3:19	Revelation 2:5

Read the following passages that indicate someone's reaction to being caught doing wrong. What, in context, indicates whether or not genuine repentance was involved?

Jonah 3:1–10	Assyrians at Jonah's preaching
Hosea 3:1–5	Hosea's wife for adultery
Genesis 9:20–27	Noah for behavior after the flood
1 Samuel 15:1–35 of Amalek	Saul for his disobedience in the matter
Luke 19:1–10	Zaccheaus, who had abused his authority as a tax collector

King Josiah (2 Kings 21:25–23:30) ended much—but not all—of the idol worship in Judah, restored the temple of God, and celebrated the Passover for the first time in many years. His reign was several years after the northern kingdom of Israel had been defeated by the Assyrians, and the remaining southern kingdom of Judah was still threatened. Read the "parable" in Jeremiah 3:6–15 and explain in your own words what is meant by verse 11, "Faithless Israel has shown herself less guilty than false Judah" (RSV).

Prayer

Read Paul's brief summary of his preaching in Acts 26:19–21. Pray for those who have repented and turned to God that they may act in accordance with that repentance.

Meditating on God's Word

David was described as a man after God's own heart (1 Sam. 13:14) and yet he was guilty of murder to hide his adultery. Read 2 Samuel 11:1–12:31 about this episode and what David himself wrote afterwards in Psalm 51. Consider what it is about David's heart that pleased God. See also 1 Chronicles 20:1–3 and 1 Kings 14:7–9; 15:3–5.

SAINTS

All the saints greet you. The grace of the
Lord Jesus Christ and the love of God and the
fellowship of the Holy Spirit be with you all.

2 Corinthians 13:13–14 (RSV)

We usually use the word "saint" in one of two ways. It may be used in the technical sense of one specially recognized (canonized) by the Roman Catholic or Eastern Orthodox church, such as Saint Bridget of Ireland or Saint Augustine. It is also used of anyone who is seen as extraordinarily good and religious: "Oh, she is a saint!" Both these meanings have developed from the usage of the word in the Bible, but both are very different from the original meaning.

In the New Testament, the saints are those people who have been sanctified (made holy) by the blood of the atoning sacrifice of Jesus Christ (Heb. 10:10). Saints are those who have confessed that Jesus is the Son of God and their Lord (Rom. 10:9) and who have been baptized in the name of the Father, the Son, and the Holy Spirit (Matt. 28:18–20) for the forgiveness of their sins (Acts 2:38). If you have been baptized into Christ, the Holy Spirit lives in you and you are one of the saints of God!

The New Testament refers to all Christians as "saints." In fact, the name "Christians" is only used three times in the New Testament, but "saints" is used over fifty times to refer to Christians in general. For example, in Acts 9 the Greek word for "saints" is used three times to refer to all the Christians in certain places: in verse 13 in Jerusalem; verse 32 in Lydda, and verse 41 in Joppa. The New International Version (1984) has "saints" in verses 13 and 32, and "believers" in verse 41. Because of the difference in the modern use of the word "saint" and the New Testament meaning of "everyone God has sanctified," the 2011 edition of the New International Version uses other terms instead of "saints."

The Greek word for "saint" is *hagios,* which can also be translated "holy" or "sanctified." (It can be a noun or an adjective.) The basic meaning of saint, sanctified, or holy is "to be set apart." God is different, set apart, and holy. He makes what belongs to him holy also (Exod. 29:43–44; Lev. 10:3; Isa. 5:16; and elsewhere).

When one becomes a Christian, he or she is set apart for service to God. This makes one different, and it means different behavior is expected, as many Scriptures teach. Some passages speak of the bad behavior and attitudes to be avoided, such as: "All impurity or covetousness must not even be named among you, as is fitting among saints" (Eph. 5:3 RSV). Other passages encourage positive actions, like welcoming and helping others "as befits the saints" (Rom. 16:2 RSV).

The concern expressed in the Old Testament that God's people be a holy people (Lev. 19:2, and many others) is repeated in the New Testament (1 Pet. 1:15–16 and elsewhere). Although each Christian is one of the saints, Jesus is the only individual called "a saint" (*hagios*). The plural noun "saints" is always used when referring to Christians, emphasizing the importance of the community formed by Christ's sanctifying work (Eph. 2:19–22). Each Christian is one of the saints—not a solitary saint alone with God, but part of the family of God living and working with brothers and sisters in Christ.

The saints we read about in the New Testament often did not act as we would expect holy people to behave. For example, Paul writes to the church in Corinth primarily to address the many problems there, including immorality. They were not living up to God's standards, and yet, they were still addressed as "the church of God which is at Corinth, even them that are sanctified in Christ Jesus, called to be saints, with all that call on the name of our Lord Jesus Christ in every place, their Lord and ours" (1 Cor. 1:2 ASV). These saints were reminded: "You were washed, you were sanctified, you were justified in the name of the Lord Jesus Christ and in the Spirit of our God" (1 Cor. 6:11 RSV). They had been set apart, but still had to learn how they should conduct themselves as the people of God rather than people of the world. Today it is still important that everyone baptized into Christ learn to live in a holy manner.

The adjective *hagios* ("holy") can be used to describe a person or a thing. John the Baptizer is called "a righteous and holy man" (Mark 6:20); the new Jerusalem is "the holy city" (Rev. 21:2). But when this word is used as a noun, it refers to Christians as people God has sanctified—the saints. A thing may be holy or not be holy. However, people who are set apart for God's service must practice holiness.

Paul addressed his letter to the Romans by saying, "to all that are in Rome, beloved of God, called to be saints" (Rom. 1:7 ASV). Most of Paul's letters begin in a similar way, with reference to the Christians as saints. For example, 2 Corinthians 1:1 (RSV), "to the church of God which is at Corinth, with all the saints who are in the whole of Acha'ia" and Philippians 1:1, "to all the saints in Christ Jesus who are at Philippi, with the bishops and deacons" (RSV). Other translations contain such wording as "God's holy people in Christ" (Phil. 1:1 TNIV 2005). The Greek word "saints" (*hagioi*) is also used in the opening greeting of Ephesians (1:1) and Colossians (1:2), although some translations use different wording.

These letters were written to every Christian in these places—not just a few "special Christians." There are many passages where it is important to realize that all Christians are saints to avoid misunderstanding the meaning: Romans 8:27, "the Spirit intercedes for the saints" (NIV84, RSV); Ephesians 4:12, "to equip the saints for the work of ministry" (RSV); Colossians 1:26, "the mystery that has been kept hidden for ages and generations, but is now disclosed to the saints" (NIV84). All Christians should hear these verses as referring to them personally. The Word of God has come to all Christians, Christ enables each one for ministry, and the Spirit intercedes for every Christian. Every one baptized into Christ becomes a part of God's glorious plan for his church and has an inheritance in heaven as one of the saints (Eph. 1:18–19).

Questions and Reflection

Have you thought of yourself as "'one of the saints" before? How do you feel about that designation for every Christian?

Consider the modern usage "St. Peter" or "St. James" and how it compares to biblical usage of word "saint." What is the same? What is different?

The letter to the Ephesians uses the Greek word for "saint" or "holy" twelve times. Look up each of these passages and consider what it teaches us about being God's holy people.

1:1	2:19	3:18
1:4	2:21	4:12
1:15	3:5	5:3
1:18	3:8	6:18

What does Exodus 19:4–6 say about how Israel became a holy nation?

What does Colossians 1:10–14 say about Christians being God's holy people?

The Apostle Paul used the word for saints in the address of most of his letters (Rom. 1:7; 1 Cor. 1:2; 2 Cor. 1:1; Eph. 1:1;

Phil. 1:1; Col. 1:2). Look up one of these in several versions to see the different ways it is translated.

What do you think is the significance of the word "saints" (or an alternative) in these passages?

Which translations do you think are "best"?

There is a whole category of Christian literature (called hagiography) for accounts of the lives of saints. Perhaps you are familiar with some historical "saints" and have read their stories. If so, how have they affected you?

If not, you may want to consider learning a little about the lives of some of these Christians from ages past:

Polycarp   Aidan of Lindisfarne
Zita of Lucca   Monica of Hippo
Cyril and Methodius   Thérèse of Lisieux

Prayer

Read Hebrews 12:1–2 and pray for strength to
avoid sin and always keep your focus on Jesus.

Meditating on God's Word

The book of Leviticus is primarily concerned with ritual purity
and holiness. Read 19:1–20:7 for sins to avoid; read chapter 23
for a list of festivals to celebrate in worshiping the Lord.

SLAVE

Paul, a slave [doulos] *of Jesus Christ,
called to be an apostle*

Romans 1:1 (CEB)

Slavery has been a harsh reality in many places through the ages. It is always a departure from the will of God. Our loving God made people in his own image and gives us freedom to choose whether we will love him in return. For one person to enslave another violates the divine order and plan. It is an expression of evil and sin in the world.

What we know of slavery from American history—kidnapping, chains, and racial oppression—is in many ways quite different from slavery in the ancient world. Various forms of slavery still exist in the shadows, illegally. In the ancient world, slavery was legal and accepted. A slave might have been of any race and was more likely to have been sold into slavery in payment of a debt than to have been captured in a war or a raid and taken away in chains.

In the Old Testament, there is little distinction between a slave and a free servant. Different Hebrew words tend to reflect the type of work a person did, rather than their status as slave or free. The most common word translated as "slave" (*ebed*) can refer to those doing hard labor (Gen. 26:19), to trusted advisors of a king (Gen. 41:38), or to members of a household trained and armed for war (Gen. 14:15). Earlier English translations (such as the Geneva Bible) tend to translate *ebed* with words for various types of servants and almost never use the word "slave" (which later translations may use). This accurately reflected the language of the time, and a society with strict class divisions and almost no social mobility, much like the ancient world.

Slaves were considered property, and they could be bought and sold. One might become a slave by being captured in war or by selling oneself in payment of a debt, but most slaves were born slaves. A household slave might serve the same family his parents had, and his children might serve there also. Sometimes in the ancient world, a slave could buy his own freedom, or he might be set free. A former slave might continue working for his former master for wages.

One's experience of slavery could vary greatly according to the work he did, his abilities (and so his usefulness), and the character of his master. The slave who nursed and raised the master's children might be loved more than some family members. The trusted slave of an influential person might have great social status and exercise considerable power in the community. Slaves who did more menial tasks had much harder lives. The status of a slave often depended more on the status, wealth, and position of the master than on the fact of being a slave.

The Old Testament has laws limiting slavery and requiring humane treatment of slaves. If a man knocks out a slave's tooth, the slave goes free (Exod. 21:27). If a man wants to marry a woman taken captive in war, he must first give her time to mourn her family, and then he is always to treat her as a wife, not as a slave (Deut. 21:10–14). Laws prohibiting work on the Sabbath applied to everyone, not just the wealthy (Deut. 5:14). Ownership of slaves was normally limited to six years; and with his freedom, the former slave was to be given provisions and means of support (Deut. 15:12–15, 18).

Often, when instructions are given about how people should view God and how they should treat one another, God is described as "the Lord your God who brought you out of the land of Egypt, out of the house of slavery" (Deut. 5:6 NASB; see also Exod. 13:14; Deut. 6:12; Judg. 6:8–9; Mic. 6:4; and elsewhere). Four of the five Books of Moses (Exodus, Leviticus, Numbers, and Deuteronomy) tell of this act of redemption that was central to the Israelites' identity. It was to be celebrated annually in the Passover festival, and it provided background for understanding Christ's redemptive act.

In New Testament times, slavery was permitted and regulated by Roman law. The legal status of a slave and a free person would be very different, even though one could not always tell which they were by a person's appearance or speech. It was not unusual for a slave to be better educated than his master. However, a slave was legal property, and he had no recourse when mistreated or abused by his master. There were many slaves in ancient Rome and many "freedmen"—former slaves who were now free.

The Greek word *doulos* means "slave," but it is sometimes translated "servant" instead. In some cases this is appropriate, but there is a different word, *diakanos*, for servant. A *diakanos* is a free person who has a specific task to do for someone else. A *doulos* is not free, but belongs to another person. The word *doulos* gives no indication of what type of work the slave might do. The term "doula" is used today of a woman who helps another woman during labor and childbirth. A doula will have some training, but is not a nurse or midwife; she provides support to the woman and her family during and after childbirth; her purpose is to help the new mother in whatever way needed. This caregiving function reflects one of the many roles of slaves in the ancient world.

Several New Testament passages that give instructions for how families should treat each other include instructions to slaves and masters. Slaves are told: "Whatever your task, work heartily, as serving the Lord and not men" (Col. 3:23 RSV; see also Eph. 6:5–8), and masters are told: "Treat your slaves justly and fairly, knowing that you also have a Master in heaven" (Col. 4:1 RSV; see also Eph. 6:9). These passages do not endorse slavery, but instruct Christians how to behave in that situation. The nature of Christianity changed the relationships between masters and slaves, and yet it was important that the conduct of Christian slaves not hurt the church's witness in the world (1Tim. 6:1–2). After the runaway slave Onesimus became a Christian, Paul sends him back to his master (Philem. 12) with a letter exhorting Philemon to receive him not as a slave, but as a beloved brother in Christ (Philem. 16).

Both the Old and the New Testament speak of slavery as an established practice, and slaves figure in many of Jesus's parables. But no Scripture promotes or defends slavery (although there have, of course, been times when slaveholders have used Scripture for their own purposes). The spread of Christianity contributed to the decline of slavery in the Roman Empire, and it is no accident that Christians have been at the forefront of movements for abolition throughout history.

Of course, it is easier to read Scripture through our own cultural lens. However, to fully understand its message, we must try to see what was said to others in a different time and place. Only then can we properly understand what is the eternal truth taught for us, as well as for the original readers.

In a world where slavery was common, Paul often refers to himself as a slave of Christ (Rom. 1:1; Phil. 1:1; Titus 1:1; and elsewhere). Other New Testament writers do also: Timothy (Phil. 1:1), James (James 1:1), Simon Peter (2 Pet. 1:1), and Jude (Jude 1). This is one way they described their total devotion to Christ. Unfortunately, *doulos* is usually translated as "servant" in these passages rather than as "slave," losing some of the richness of meaning. A servant has a job to do for someone else; a slave belongs to another person and his identity is bound up in that of his master. Because a slave's well-being depends on his pleasing his master, his conduct tends to reflect the desires and the character of his master. Being a slave for Christ is the highest calling one can have. To belong to Christ defines who one is and influences all a Christian does.

Paul understood that one who yields to sin becomes a slave to sin. But grace gives an alternative. "When you were slaves of sin, you were free in regard to righteousness. . . . But now that you have been set free from sin and have become slaves of God, the return you get is sanctification and its end, eternal life" (Rom. 6:20, 22 RSV). Paul knew that he was "bought at a price" (1 Cor. 6:20 NIV; see also 1 Cor. 7:20–24) and was bound to do the Lord's will in everything. He was happy to belong to Christ and identify himself as a slave of Christ.

Questions and Reflection

Most of us know slavery as a shameful part of our nation's history or as a frightening evil suffered by some in other countries. We are very uncomfortable with thinking of ourselves as slaves. How do you feel about Christians being called "slaves" [translations mine] of God?

> Acts 4:29 ". . . give to Your slaves . . ."
> Romans 6:22 ". . . having become slaves of God . . ."
> Revelation 7:3 ". . . until we have sealed the slaves of God . . ."

What do you think about these passages?

Do you know hymns that address God as "master"?

Read Galatians 4:3–8 and tell (in your own words) how the analogy of slavery is used in this passage.

Throughout history Christians have, as an expression of their faith, spearheaded movements to abolish slavery, as did William Wilberforce, who was portrayed in the movie *Amazing Grace*. Other examples of Christians who worked to free slaves or abolish slavery include:

Eligius (7th cent. French)
Henri Gregoire (18th–19th cent. French)
Anselm of Canterbury (11th cent. British)
Thomas Clarkson (18th–19th cent. English)
John of Matha (12th cent. French)
Harriet Beecher Stowe (19th cent. American)
John Woolman (18th cent. American)
David Livingston (19th cent. Scottish)

What passages/biblical principles do you think might have led to their conviction/efforts?

In the mid-nineteenth century, when slavery was a much-debated issue in the United States, some preachers used the existence of slavery in the Bible and the fact that slaves are told to obey their masters (1 Tim. 6:1–2 and elsewhere) as an argument in favor of slavery. Was this a legitimate interpretation of Scripture? Why or why not?

To what extent do you think their cultural setting influenced their interpretation of Scripture?

How does our cultural setting today change the way we read Scripture?

Prayer

Read Luke 4:16–21. Say a prayer of praise and thanksgiving for Jesus.

Meditating on God's Word

Read 1 Corinthians 8:1–11:1 paying special attention to the themes of freedom and belonging.

SUBMIT

Submit to one another out of reverence for Christ.

Ephesians 5:21 (NIV)

Growing up in the church, I heard a lot about submission—and not as a dirty word either. Ours was a Bible-reading, Bible-believing, Bible-obeying church, so we all knew submission was a virtue. But it is doubtful that anyone quite knew what submission is. We heard that a wife should submit to her husband, but were not really clear on what that meant. Most of the other passages on submission were overlooked, so we did not have a very complete picture. The Greek word for "submit" or "submission" occurs thirty-eight times in the New Testament. Only seven times does it refer specifically to women. Clearly "submission" needs further study.

The New American Heritage Dictionary defines "submit" as "to yield to the opinion or authority of another." This is something everyone does every day, although we do not necessarily think that we are submitting when we do it. At work, we do things "the company way" even when we are pretty sure there is a better way. We comply with government rules when filing taxes or renewing a driver's license. We conform to safety regulations. Sometimes we submit a proposal or other document that we developed, but are now making available for another's approval and use. In each of these cases, we set aside our own preferences and desires to do what someone else wants us to, and we do it more for our own benefit than for anyone else's. That is what it means to submit.

There are many passages in the Bible where someone is in submission to someone else. Here are a few:

Jesus to Mary and Joseph	Luke 2:51
Christ to God	1 Corinthians 15:28
Everyone to God	Hebrews 12:9; James 4:7
Christians to political authorities	Titus 3:1; 1 Peter 2:13
Church to Christ	Ephesians 5:24
Christians to leaders	1 Corinthians 16:15–16
Younger to older	1 Peter 5:5
Servants to masters	Titus 2:9; 1 Peter 2:18
Spirit of prophets to prophets	1 Corinthians 14:32
Demons to Jesus's disciples	Luke 10:17, 20

Notice that these passages always speak of submitting to others, never of keeping someone in submission. You cannot make me submit—if I do not chose to submit, you may be able to subjugate me, but I will not have submitted. In spite of this, you have probably heard it said that a Christian man should "keep his wife in submission." Anyone who says this clearly does not understand what it means to submit (or what the Bible teaches about marriage!). If a husband subjugates his wife, she may be in a state of subjugation (which is sometimes called submission), but by taking away her choice in the matter he has made it impossible for her to submit as the Bible teaches. One can only submit if it is an action freely chosen by the one submitting.

This may be clearer if we look at the Greek word that can be translated either "subjugate" or "submit" depending on the form of the word used. The word *hupotasso* means "to subjugate," "to conquer," or "to make (someone) subject to (someone else)." It is used this way in Philippians 3:21, "the power which enables him even *to subject* all things to himself" (RSV—italics added), or "the power that enables him *to bring* everything *under* his *control*" (NIV—italics added). This is what we call the *active voice* of the verb, where someone does something to someone else. In this verse, it is Christ who has the power to bring everything under his control.

There is also a *passive voice* of the verb, where something is done to someone. The passive form of *hupotasso* means "to be (made) subject to" or "to be (or have been) subjugated." This usage is in 1 Peter 3:22, "angels and authorities and powers *being made subject* unto him" (KJV—italics added). The New International Version translates this verse as "with angels, authorities and powers *in submission* to him." In this case, Christ is not actively subjugating anything, but things are already in a state of having been made subject to him; the "powers" did not do anything—it was done to them. Sometimes this passive use of *hupotasso* is switched to the active "submit" in English: "heavenly messengers and authorities and powers *submit* to His supremacy" (VOICE), but the emphasis is still on the state of being, rather than on action being taken.

Both passive and active forms of *hupotasso* are seen in Romans 8:20: "for creation *was subjected* to futility, not of its own will but by the will of him who *subjected* it in hope" (RSV—italics added). Creation had no choice in the matter—God took action that affected creation.

Passages that use the active or passive voice only account for about a third of the times *hupotasso* is used in the New Testament. Twenty-six times it is used in what is called the *middle voice*. English does not have the middle voice; it only has the active and passive voices. But just as there is a great difference between conquering and being conquered, so is the meaning of the middle voice different than the active or the passive voice. The middle voice is used when someone does something that has an effect on the one taking action. It can emphasize the subject's participation in both what is done and the outcome. It involves actively doing something, but what is done is done to or for oneself.

The same word in Greek sometimes has a different meaning in the active and the middle voices. For example, the word for "make peace" means stop fighting and agree to be peaceful if it is in the middle voice, but in the active voice it means to act as a mediator to bring about peace between others. The mediator is acting for others, not himself, so the active voice is used; those making peace are taking action and enjoying the results of their own actions, so the middle voice is used. The word for "to clothe" is used in the active voice in Luke 15:22: "Bring the best robe and *put it on* him" (NIV) and in the middle voice in Luke 12:22: "Do not worry about . . . what you *will wear*" (NIV). The active voice is used when someone does something to another; the middle voice is used when someone is participating in the results of his own actions. Because English does not have a middle voice, it is sometimes difficult to know how to translate it.

The middle voice is used in Romans 13:1, 5: "Let every person *submit* to the governing authorities. For there is no authority except from God. . . . Therefore, one must *submit*, not only to avoid God's wrath but also for the sake of conscience" (translation mine). Here, "to submit" is clearly a choice people must make for themselves, an act of will—not something forced on one by another. It is the middle voice of *hupotasso* that is used when the meaning is "submit," as in the passages listed at the beginning of this discussion. In Greek, sometimes the passive ("be subjugated") and middle ("submit oneself") of *hupotasso* look similar, but the meaning is very different. A careful look at the context makes it clear whether the meaning is passive or middle voice. If it is passive voice, something has been done to someone (one person is subjugated by another). When it is the middle voice, someone is actively involved in what is done or its outcome (one chooses to submit).

The Greek lexicon by Arndt and Gingrich defines this use of *hupotasso* in the middle voice as "voluntary yielding in love."[2] Every time it is specified that women are to submit to someone, it is wives submitting to their own husbands (never to any other men). And every time wives are told to submit to

---

[2] William F. Arndt and F. Wilbur Gingrich, *A Greek-English Lexicon of the New Testament and Other Early Christian Literature* (Chicago: University of Chicago Press, 1957), s. v. "hupotasso."

their own husbands it is in the middle voice (Eph. 5:21–22, 24; Col. 3:18; Titus 2:5; 1 Pet. 3:1, 5). These passages encourage wives to lovingly yield to their husbands. Wives choose to take action, and they participate in the results of their actions. These same passages also give other instructions to husbands ("love . . . as Christ loved the church and gave himself up for her," Eph. 5:25; "do not be harsh," Col. 3:19; "live considerately with your wives," 1 Pet. 3:7 RSV), which men sometimes find equally difficult to follow. Yet following God's way always brings blessings.

Many people in the world today, and even in the church, think submission is out of date and out of place in the modern world. If their idea of a wife submitting to her husband is the same as a husband "lording it over" his wife (and making her life miserable), then that is certainly out of place in the church, too. However, when both husband and wife understand and practice what God means by submission it leads to a beautiful relationship. Ephesians 5:18–21 portrays submitting to one another as characteristic of those filled with the Holy Spirit.

Those who think submission is only about how men treat their wives are mistaken on two counts. Submission is about order and peaceful relationships in the world and the church, not just in marriage. Additionally, submission is, by definition, something one freely chooses to do, not something someone can demand of another. Some misunderstandings of biblical teaching on submission come from the difficulty of interpreting and practicing these Scriptures, and some come from the misuse of Scripture. Wrong teaching on submission has led to much frustration and discord. However, if one learns what "submitting" means in the Bible, then it can contribute to very good situations.

God who made us, knows us, and loves us tells us to submit. Lovingly yield (submit) to God; submit to those who are older; submit to Christian leaders; submit to political authorities; and submit to one another. When we actively choose to submit to God's way, we participate in the outcome of peace in our world, goodwill, and calm.

Questions and Reflection

What do you see as the difference between "obey" and "submit"? How might it be possible to do one but not the other?

How does submission take different forms according to the one to whom one submits?

What might be different about submission to civil authorities in a democracy or in a dictatorship?

What about submitting to different employers with different ideas about how to do business?

Are you more comfortable describing a good marriage as one where husband and wife are equal, making all decisions together ("egalitarian") or as one where the husband has leadership responsibility ("complementary")?

How does biblical teaching on love, respect, and submission fit each model?

Consider these two definitions:

> submission = setting aside one's own will to do another's will for *one's own* benefit

> *agape* (love) = setting aside one's own will to do another's will for *the other's* benefit

> How do each of these play a role in your relationships within your family?

Which teaching on submission do you find personally more challenging: to God, to government, to church leaders, to those who are older?

Consider the words to the hymn "None of Self and All of Thee" or "All to Jesus I Surrender," and discuss what is said about the difficulty and the blessings of submitting to God.

Prayer

Read James 4:1–10 and pray for the grace
and humility to draw nearer to God in your
mind, your heart, and your actions.

Meditating on God's Word

Keeping in mind the definition of submission as "voluntary yielding in love," read Romans 14:1–15:13 on the relationships between those who are "weak" in faith and those who are "strong." Make a list of instructions given specifically to each group and a list of instructions given to everyone.

TALENT

One who owed him ten thousand talents was brought to him.

Matthew 18:24 (NASB)

The English word "talent" has two unrelated meanings. One refers to the natural abilities of a person, as in the sentence: "She has a talent for playing the piano." In other words, playing the piano is easier for her and she is able to play the piano better than most people. The other meaning of "talent" refers to a very large amount of money—the largest unit of money in the ancient world. The Greek word *talanta* and the Latin word *talenta* (from which our word "talent" comes) both refer to a sum of money measured by its weight. In Scripture, the word "talent" refers to money, not to a skill or ability. The parable discussed below is one of many passages that reminds us that attitudes toward money and how wealth is used are spiritual matters.

Different ways of comparing the value of a talent with modern units of money have been tried in the past. One way is to figure the value of that weight of silver. By this method, estimates range from 960 to more than 1,000 dollars; or from 344 to 600 British pounds. Of course, these estimates are affected by the rates of exchange at the time of translation and need to be adjusted every few years. The value of any given unit of money tended to be much more stable in the ancient world than it is today. Exact equivalents are difficult to calculate.

Another way of estimating the value of a talent is to figure the length of time necessary to earn the money. The Revised Standard Version and New International Version identify a drachma this way in the footnotes on Luke 15:8–9; a drachma would be the usual daily wage for most workers. (A drachma was the Greek coin; the Roman equivalent was a denarius.) One hundred denarii (or drachmae) would be worth about three months' salary. That is how much one servant owed the other servant. Six thousand drachmae were equal to one talent.[3] This can be used to figure how much money could be earned by an unskilled worker today in the same amount of time required to earn a given sum in the ancient world.

Understanding what Jesus said about the money will help you to grasp the meaning of the parable of the unforgiving servant (Matt. 18:23–35). A king decided to settle accounts with those who owed him money. A man was brought before him who owed him ten thousand talents. (Ten thousand was the largest numerical unit in the ancient world—it was sometimes

---

[3] Everett Ferguson, *Backgrounds of Early Christianity*, 3rd ed. (Grand Rapids: Eerdmans, 2003), 93.

used in much the way we sometimes say "billions and billions" or "trillions.") The king, knowing the man could not repay him, ordered him to be sold along with his family, and the money applied to his debt. The man begged the king not to do that, and he promised to repay all of the debt. Those listening to Jesus tell this parable probably laughed when they heard what the servant promised to repay; they understood what an unbelievable amount of money ten thousand talents was. The king took pity on him and forgave the debt—all of it. The man then went out, found a fellow laborer who owed him one hundred denarii and demanded full payment, even after he had been forgiven a much larger sum. When the king heard about it, he had the servant thrown into prison to be tortured until he paid it all. But the ten thousand talents he owed was an unimaginable debt. The use of the largest possible number and the largest possible monetary unit emphasized the impossibility of repayment.

Now for the math. (If you have trouble with the math, ask a fifth grader.) Start with the typical salary for a day laborer in New Testament times—the minimum wage, we might call it. In the Roman world, that would be a denarius. (See Matt. 20:2.) The comparable amount of money in the Greek world was a drachma. One servant owed the other servant one hundred denarii, or about three months' salary. A significant amount, but an amount that could be repaid over time.

There are six thousand denarii (or drachmai) in a talent; so the first servant would need to work for six thousand days to earn one talent. To see how many years are in six thousand days, divide 6,000 by 365. Your answer will be just under sixteen and a half. That is the number of years it would take a day laborer to earn one talent. But remember, he owed ten thousand talents, not just one. So multiply 16 by 10,000. Your answer is 160,000! That is the minimum number of years it would take for the servant to earn the vast sum of ten thousand talents owed to the king. In fact, it would take him much longer, because he has not eaten yet! Nor has he paid for any of his normal living expenses. He owed the king all the money he could earn in over 160,000 years! Even if he could earn a salary much higher than average, he could not possibly make that much money in several lifetimes.

This parable about the unforgiving, or unmerciful, servant shows how impossible it would be for the servant to pay his huge debt, although he promised to repay all of it. It is not really about economics, but about forgiveness. The king used this debt to show kindness; the first servant received the kindness, but was unwilling to extend it to the other servant.

The lesson for us is that we also owe a debt we cannot pay. Our debt is not of money, but of our sins, and only the Lord, our merciful Savior can forgive our debt, and it was the death of Jesus on the cross that made forgiveness possible. The exaggeration in this parable emphasizes the overflowing abundance of God's forgiveness and mercy.

We must not be like the ungrateful servant who tried to force the man who owed him only three month's salary to pay it all, even after he had been forgiven such a huge amount. If we expect to be forgiven, we must forgive those who are our debtors. In the words of the prayer in Matthew 6:12: "And forgive us our debts, as we also have forgiven our debtors" (NIV).

Questions and Reflection

Look at the following passages on wealth and poverty. List the attitudes and actions expected of wealthy disciples, and list the attitudes and actions expected of the righteous poor.

1 Timothy 6:6–10, 17–19   2 Corinthians 9:9–15

Use a concordance or online search tool to see what the book of Proverbs says about "wealth."

Following are several types of requests for forgiveness and examples of each. Choose one passage from each category and analyze what forgiveness meant in that example.

Intercession for a group	Individual requests to God	Between individuals
Exodus 32:9–14	Exodus 10:16–17	Genesis 50:15–21
Job 42:7–9	2 Kings 5:18–19	1 Samuel 15:24–26
Daniel 9:4–19	Psalm 19:12–13	2 Corinthians 2:5–11

Look at the following passages and consider what is the relationship between God's forgiving us and our forgiving each other:

Matthew 6:14–15   Colossians 3:13–14

In each of the following passages, what is the reason God forgives people?

Numbers 14:19   Matthew 26:28
Psalm 25:11   Acts 2:38
Jeremiah 36:3   Hebrews 9:22
Micah 7:18   1 John 1:9

In the following passages there is (or will be) no forgiveness. What reasons are given in each for the lack of forgiveness from God?

Deuteronomy 29:18–20   2 Kings 24:3–4
Joshua 24:19–20   Jeremiah 5:7–9

What are your favorite songs or hymns about God's grace and forgiveness?

Prayer

Read James 2:1–7 for ideas about how to
pray for yourself and for those you love
most to have godly attitudes toward other
people and toward wealth. Pray.

Meditating on God's Word

Read the Old Testament book of Hosea (14 chapters, most of them quite short), noting the themes of forgiveness and faithfulness/unfaithfulness.

ZEALOUS

It is fine to be zealous, provided the purpose is good.

Galatians 4:18a (NIV)

" Zeal" is an English word that comes straight from the Greek *zelos*. To be "zealous" or "full of zeal" means to be eager, devoted, and to give energetic support. It is not to be confused with "jealous," which can refer to the careful protection of what is one's own, or to the resentment of someone who has something coveted or who is seen as a rival. Although both "jealous" and "zealous" come from the same Greek word, their meanings in English are quite different.

"Jealousy" is usually a negative word, referring to emotions that often motivate sinful behavior: "Where there is jealousy and selfishness, there is also disorder and every kind of evil" (James 3:16 GNT). Jealousy is a part of love (Song of Sol. 8:6) and feelings of jealousy are natural and appropriate when one is betrayed by a spouse, even though sometimes those feelings come when there is nothing in the spouse's behavior to justify them (Num. 5:14). When God is described as a "jealous God" it is because worship belongs to him alone, and it should never be given to anyone or anything else. "You shall worship no other god, for the LORD, whose name is Jealous, is a jealous God" (Exod. 34:14 RSV; see also Exod. 20:5; Nah. 1:2–3). The apostle Paul speaks in a similar way about the Corinthians:

> I am jealous for you with a godly jealousy. I prom-
> ised you to one husband, to Christ, so that I might
> present you as a pure virgin to him. But I am afraid
> that . . . your minds may somehow be led astray
> from your sincere and pure devotion to Christ.
> (2 Cor. 11:2–3 NIV)

Paul's concern is not a sinful jealousy, but rather the same concern that God has that his people worship God alone.

The word "zealous" refers not so much to an emotion as to an attitude of devotion and eager support. (It can be used to translate Greek words other than *zelos*.) This sort of enthusiasm is commended and encouraged in many ways in Scripture.

"Never be lacking in zeal" (Rom. 12:11 NIV)

"who has proved to us in many ways that he is zealous" (2 Cor. 8:22 NIV)

"a people of his own who are zealous for good deeds" (Titus 2:14 RSV)

"so be zealous and repent" (Rev. 3:19 RSV)

Of course, one can be zealous for the wrong things. The Corinthian church was eager for spiritual gifts—especially the exciting ones like speaking in tongues. But Paul tells them (1 Cor. 12:31; 14:12) that they should instead be zealous for things that build up (edify) the church: teaching and knowledge, thoughtful songs and prayers, meaningful praise and thanksgiving (14:5–6, 15–17). To be a good thing, zeal must be based on knowledge and accompanied by submission to God's standard of righteousness (Rom. 10:2–3).

We have now come from A (Abba) to Z (zealous). While we have not been comprehensive, our prayer is that what has been included will help you want to understand the Bible better and also see some ways to study the Bible. Our purpose has been to bring you closer to our Lord and Savior. As you draw nearer and learn more about God, you will see more things that you will want to change in your life in order to please the Lord and show your love for him. May God bless you with wisdom and understanding as you continue to study his holy, inspired Word.

THE NEXT STEPS

There is so much to be gained from continuing study and practice of God's Word. It is our prayer that we have helped you look more carefully at words not in your everyday vocabulary and that studying them has helped you learn of God. If you have read through this book and worked through most of the exercises, then you have had good instruction and practice in how to study, as well as occasion to ponder what it means to live as a Christian.

We encourage you to continue your journey of faith. Read Scripture regularly. Read it for the big picture, and allow it to do to you what it was meant to do to those who heard it for the first time. Cherish the small details. Allow the Holy Spirit to train you in righteousness.

Following are a few recommendations to **PRACTICE** Bible study:

PRAY. Always begin with prayer. Pray that God will open the eyes of your heart so that you will understand what he wants to say to you.

READ AND WRITE. Read the passage through quickly and jot down notes on anything that seems strange to you. Sometimes we read or hear Scriptures so often that they begin to sound familiar and we start to think we know what they mean even if we don't. Making a "strange" list will remind you later of what you wanted to study further.

AGAIN. Read the passage several times. Let the words soak in. Consider what it might mean, and the limits of what it could mean. Take a look at the context: What comes before and after, and how does this passage fit into its context?

CHECK OTHER TRANSLATIONS. Sometimes the translators have difficulty deciding which word should be used, and reading more than one version will help give you a more complete picture of what the original might mean.

TAKE IN DETAILS. Focus on individual words that seem significant in this passage. What exactly do they mean? Where else are they used in Scripture and what do they mean there?

INVESTIGATE TOPICS. Consider other passages that relate to the same topics as the one you are studying. What do they have to say on the subject, and how does that enhance your understanding of the primary passage?

CONSULT COMMENTARIES. You may want to see what others have said about this passage. Commentary authors usually have much experience in Bible study, interpretation, and teaching. Those with extensive knowledge of the original languages and the cultural setting of Scripture are especially valuable sources of insight. But remember that commentaries are not Scripture, and they can be wrong. Always study a passage for yourself first, and then if you want to consult what others say about it you have some basis for discerning whether what they say seems right.

ENDEAVOR TO OBEY. Pray that God will enable you to act in accordance with the Scripture you have studied. Pray that when you need it, the Holy Spirit will bring to your remembrance what you have learned and give you the strength to follow it. Praise God for his Blessed Word!

Perhaps you have already encountered the term *exegesis*. It may sound intimidating, but it is just a word from the Greek meaning "to lead out." It refers to the process of allowing biblical texts to provide their own interpretation, rather than reading one's own ideas into the text or using the text to prove things it may not really say. Exegesis involves studying the details of a text (language and grammar) and its context (literary and historical) to help determine the most likely meaning for the original readers before making applications for the present day.

In reading through this book, you have practiced the skills used in exegesis: using a dictionary and concordance, learning to examine context, and identifying major themes of a passage. You need never shy away from the word "exegesis" again, because you have begun to do it. But truly, the hardest part of Bible study is never in understanding what it says. Once the Scripture has been interpreted to the best of one's ability, it is necessary to hear what its message is for us today, and to obey. As difficult as some passages of Scripture may be to understand, the hardest part of Bible study will always be living what has been learned.

No doubt you already have in mind passages you would like to study more closely or books of the Bible you would like to read next. May God bless you in that pursuit. If you would like recommendations for further study, here are a few suggestions.

For "big picture" readings:

The Letter of James: practical advice on Christian living.

Genesis: this first book of Moses shows God as creator and tells the story of the first of his chosen people.

Deuteronomy: this last of the five books of Moses summarizes the Exodus, the wilderness wanderings, and what God expects from the people he has redeemed.

Amos: the words of a simple man God called to warn a nation to repent.

Luke and Acts: a two-volume work on the life of Christ and his continuing ministry in the church.

The Fourth Book of Psalms: Psalms 90–106, for a
variety of emotions and words of praise.

For shorter passages to study in detail:

John 1:1–18 Christ in the world

Mark 4:1–20 parable of the sower

Matthew 22:23–33 Jesus and the Sadducees

Luke 12:22–34 Jesus teaches about God's care

Colossians 3:5–17 putting off the old and putting on the
new

Ephesians 5:1–20 walking in God's way

Titus 3:3–8 on new life in Christ

For specific words to study:

"freedom" in the New Testament—from what and for
what

"in Christ" (exact phrase) in Ephesians

"justice/just" in Deuteronomy or in Jeremiah

"mercy" in the Gospels (Matthew, Mark, Luke,
and John)

"one another" in Romans

"praise" in the Psalms

"remember" in Deuteronomy and Hebrews

"remnant" in Haggai and Zechariah

"return" in Isaiah

"sanctify" in Leviticus and Romans

"visit" in Acts

"worthy" in the New Testament letters (Romans
through Jude)

It takes very little understanding to become a follower of Christ. It takes a lifetime walking in faith with the Holy Spirit to develop wisdom and maturity. It will take eternity to fully know God.

NANCY FERGUSON AND ANN DOYLE

CPSIA information can be obtained
at www.ICGtesting.com
Printed in the USA
FSOW02n1902020417
32557FS